GLASS BY GALLÉ

The cutting and polishing studio of the Gallé glassworks, *c.*1904

GLASS BY GALLE

ALASTAIR DUNCAN   GEORGES DE BARTHA

with 357 illustrations, 93 in colour

Harry N. Abrams, Inc.,
Publishers, New York

To Vincent

Library of Congress Cataloging in Publication Data

Duncan, Alastair, 1942–
  Glass by Gallé.

  Bibliography: p.
  Includes index.
  1. Gallé, Emile, 1846–1904.   2. Glassware –
France – History – 19th century.   3. Decoration
and ornament – France – Art nouveau.
I. Gallé, Emile, 1846–1904.   II. De Bartha,
Georges.   III. Title.
NK5198.G27D86   1984   748.294   84-385
ISBN 0-8109-0986-3

Printed and bound in Japan by Dai Nippon

Contents

Introduction

This book does not provide a history of Gallé himself. Several recent biographies chronicle the family business, Emile's birth in Nancy on 4 May 1846, his upbringing, and his training at Burgun, Schwerer & Cie in Meisenthal. In 1870 he was, by his own admission, an undereducated and underprivileged young man, yet by the time of his death from leukemia on 23 September 1904 at the age of 58, he had become the era's peerless master of glassmaking. The intention here is to examine the decorative influences and glass techniques which were responsible for this transformation.

Nothing even remotely comparable to Gallé's accomplishments had been achieved in the history of European glass. Comparison with the Bohemian and Venetian exhibits at the 1900 Exposition Universelle – still fundamentally eighteenth-century in shape and decoration – shows the distance Gallé had travelled in the sixteen short years after his first tentative break with tradition at the 1884 Exposition.

The influences which inspired Gallé can be traced in the evolution of his glassware. From a technical standpoint, early works were in clear or translucent crystal (for example, *clair-de-lune*), their shapes usually classical. Later works were opaque and multicoloured, their forms naturalistic. To decorate his early works, Gallé drew on the popular themes of the period: Islamic arabesques and calligraphy; Greco-Roman mythology and medieval folklore; seventeenth-century Dutch landscapes; Egyptian iconography; Oriental woodcuts and a host of other influences readily evident in the illustrations in this book. Later glassware had its shape adapted to its theme. Vases decorated with lilies became lily-shaped. Mushroom lamps brought the concept to full embodiment.

Gallé accepted glass – a capricious yet noble and richly plastic material – as the conveyor of his dreams and aspirations as early as the 1860s, at a time when its potential was quite unrealized. Endless experimentation followed, much of it fruitless. Each discovery generated new possibilities, each failure re-evaluation. The functions of the chemist and glass artisan merged, their skills mutually dependent. Gallé's creativity and indefatigable energy proved infectious to his team of glass exponents, buoying them up, with each technical breakthrough, for the next challenge. This was often the annual salon of the Société Nationale des Beaux-Arts at the Champ-de-Mars in Paris, where an entrant's yearly progress was measured against that of his competitors. Gallé came to these occasions thoroughly prepared, often submitting extensive Notes in advance to the exhibition's Jury to ensure that the full extent of his technical innovations was comprehended and appreciated.

   Many of these Notes appear in *Ecrits pour l'art*, Gallé's collected writings published by his widow in 1908. The book tabulates his inventions in glass, ceramics and furniture, and provides fascinating insights into the man's intelligence and boundless interests. His knowledge of horticulture alone, made evident in the book's initial chapters, is sufficient to qualify Gallé as an eminently cultivated man. The later essays show his deep religious and poetic sentiments and awakening social conscience. Today, as one drives through the drab streets of Nancy, identical to those of a host of other industrial centres and railheads in Lorraine and southern Germany, one can only marvel at the fortuitous series of events which steered Gallé out of such anonymity and into international prominence.

   Gallé's love and knowledge of botany requires more than a passing nod. Early tuition under Professor D. A. Godron, author of *La Flore française* and *La Flore lorraine* sparked a profound love and rapid expertise. Gallé's twenty-six-page report on the horticultural exhibits at the 1878 Exposition Universelle, published in *Le Bulletin de la Société Centrale d'Horticulture de Nancy*, shows his encyclopaedic knowledge of flowers. The report is longer even than his glass, ceramics and

A studio sketch for a carafe, tumbler and matching underplate, depicting water lilies (source: The Corning Museum of Glass)

furniture Notes, themselves tendentious, to the Juries at the 1884 and 1889 exhibitions. They do explain, however, in their detailed scholarship and intellectualism, why Gallé could recreate such a range of spectacular blooms in glass. His sketches of orchids, published in *La Lorraine Artiste* in 1904 and reproduced here, show how easily he transferred his working knowledge of flowers on to paper, and from there to glass. A close working relationship with the Nancy botanist and geneticist, Victor Lemoine, who was especially renowned for a new species of primula, and with Charles Schulze, Gallé's own gardener at La Garenne, the family home, filled his spare time.

Roger Marx, Inspector General of French Museums and an irrepressible Gallé publicist since his earliest days, stressed this bond with nature in an obituary in *Le Bulletin des Sociétés Artistiques de l'Est*:

> He was an exquisitely sensitive poet, who lived in the midst of nature in a state of perpetual excitement, drawing decorative ideas from this great mistress of all artists and developing them through his own fertile imagination. The flora and fauna of his own region were the source of thousands of delicate and ingenious images, on which he elaborated with wonderful spirit.

Nature was unquestionably Gallé's primary source of inspiration, as he stressed in a Note to the 1884 Exposition: 'The Jury will certainly notice that whereas Nature is always my point of departure, I try to free myself from it in time to achieve my own personal character and emphasis.' Gallé drew not only on the flora of the Lorraine countryside, but on its entire zoological community. Bats, insects and butterflies became decorative accents to the blossoms which bloomed in profusion on glass and wood alike. An interesting story survives of how the umbel plant became a favourite Gallé motif. In the early 1890s, one of the firm's designers, a M.

Estaud, took a customary stroll through the nearby forests in search of rare plants. Momentarily lost, he found himself in a bog confronted by a large plant, nearly ten foot tall, with dagger-shaped leaves, crenellated stem and umbellated fruit. M. Estaud manfully dragged it back to the glassworks, placing it in the corner by his bench. From this discovery was born a highly successful series of designs for vases, lamps and marquetry furniture.

If nature dominated Gallé's thoughts, it was followed closely by two other passions – literature and symbolism. Poetry was the gateway to Gallé's dreams. An omnivorous reader from childhood, he drew on a wealth of literary sources to inspire his works in glass. The Chapter on *verreries parlantes* examines these innumerable influences. Victor Hugo's philosophical views on society, religion and justice, in particular, affected Gallé deeply, as did the Romantic poets. The writings of history's great men-of-letters – French, English and Roman alike – were also absorbed, to be recalled when a quotation or sentiment best served the mood to be evoked in glass.

Closest to Gallé's own sentiments were the Symbolist poets, especially Maurice Maeterlinck, Comte Robert de Montesquiou-Fezensac and, on occasion, Charles Baudelaire. Montesquiou's prose, in particular, had for Gallé a richly appealing sensuality. Here the link to nature was, of course, direct, and Gallé became an immediate disciple.

Gallé gave an address on 'Le Décor symbolique' to the Academie de Stanislas on 17 May 1900. The speech was characteristically thorough, punctuated liberally with verses from Baudelaire, Hugo, Valmore and Bouchor. Gallé defined symbolism in art, poetry and religion as:

> the representation of something, usually abstract, by a conventional equivalent, a sign whose meaning is agreed among the initiated. In decoration, on a vase, medal, statue,

painting, relief or temple, just as in poetry, song or mime, it is always a matter of translating or evoking an idea by an image.

Later in the speech, the symbolism of various flora was touched on; the orchid, for example, evoked:

an unimaginable richness and strangeness of forms, substances, perfumes, colours, caprices, sensual pleasures and disturbing mysteries.

Two less well known speeches, published in *La Lorraine Artiste*, were equally ardent. The first, in 1893, was entitled 'Allocution prononcée à la conférence sur Puvis de Chavannes'; the second was delivered at the 1902 conference on Paul Verlaine, 'Instantanés pris au concours de la Croix de Bourgogne'.

The above touch only on Gallé's primary sources of inspiration. Many peripheral interests remain undocumented to this day. A hunt through the archives of the Nancy public library provided further insights into this most complex of men: an 1884 economic treatise entitled 'Considérations à propos de notre commerce extérieur', in which Gallé, listing himself as an industrialist, laid out his proposals for increased foreign trade (that is, outside of Alsace-Lorraine). Elsewhere, early thoughts on such disparate topics as the architecture of Nancy and pantheism were published in obscure local journals. Gallé's infinite variety of interests defies categorization.

The glassworks grew steadily from the early 1870s until 1885, whereafter commissions increased sharply, due in part to Gallé's exposure at the 1884 and 1889 Expositions. Demand began to outstrip supply. Output was limited suddenly by the fact that pieces were entirely handcrafted, each a creation monitored by the lengthy glassblowing, enamelling, or engraving process. Gallé turned for help to his erstwhile

The house where Gallé was born, corner of rue Saint-Dizier and rue de la Faïencerie, Nancy

A view of Gallé looking out over the garden at La Garenne; to his right, a monumental amphora vase with wrought-iron mounts

training ground, Burgun, Schwerer & Cie, ordering blanks (undecorated glassware) to be decorated by his own artisans. This helped to accelerate production. Correspondence obtained recently by the Corning Museum of Glass between Gallé and Désiré Christian at Burgun, Schwerer & Cie corroborates these commissions. Gallé provided detailed technical specifications on both the shapes and the composition of the glass to be manufactured by the Meisenthal firm. His adoption in the mid-1880s of the acid-etching technique (Chapter 10), hugely reluctant but practical, freed further valuable time for commissions from the widening circle of influential clients, both private and state, eager to obtain a glass *objet d'art* from the fashionable Nancy glassmaker.

A series of prestigious commissions was afforded by the visit to Lorraine in 1893 of a Russian naval delegation headed by the Tsar's envoy, the Grand-Duke Constantine. The editor of *La Lorraine Artiste*, Goutière Vernolle, raised 50,000 f. in the three contiguous provinces of Meurthe-et-Moselle, la Meuse and Vosges to commission a 'Gold Book', as a gift from Lorraine to Imperial Russia. The two nations formed a spiritual alliance against a common aggressor, Germany. Gallé, his patriotic zeal awakened by the painful memory of his mobilization and service in the 1870 Franco-Prussian war, responded with the creation of a marquetry table entitled *Flore de Lorraine*, on which the book was to be placed. The top was inlaid in polychromed veneers with indigenous flora – myosotis, ferns, oaks, conifers, periwinkles, gentians, etc. A caveat inlaid along its border cautioned the unwary against future hegemony: 'Gardez les coeurs qu'avez gagnés.'

The bond between Lorraine and Russia thus firmly forged, a brisk cultural exchange followed. Gallé was commissioned to create several vases for the Imperial family: two engraved models handsomely mounted in gold by Falize for the Tsarina (*c.*1896) and a slender cornet with a Fabergé silver mount for the Grand-Duke Sergé. None of these appears to have survived the Revolution; a recent trip to the vaults in the Hermitage by a Gallé collector failed to reveal any glassware of merit.

There were relatively few *pièces uniques*. One was the vase *La Soude* for the Belgian chemist Ernest Solvay in 1902, its base designed as a pile of soda crystals. Another was the vase dedicated in 1896 to Gallé's long-time friend and collaborator, Victor Prouvé, in celebration of the latter's nomination to the Order of the Legion of Honour. The seventieth anniversary of Louis Pasteur's birth generated a commission from the Ecole Normale Supérieure as a presentation to the scientist. Exhibited at the 1893 Champ-de-Mars, the piece is now in the Pasteur Museum, Paris. Gallé described its conception and creation, replete with laboratory instruments, chemical vapours, microbes and inscribed homage, in a detailed article in *La Revue encyclopédique* in 1893.

Most commissioned pieces were subsequently reproduced in limited editions of four or five, such as two vases for the magistrate Henri Hirsch, for years a major client. Another admirer was Eugène Corbin, publisher of *Art et industrie*, whose long patronage culminated in his 1935 gift to the city of his collection of Ecole de Nancy works of art.

The July 1909 issue of *Art et industrie* listed fifty-six donors to a retrospective exhibition of Gallé glassware at the Musée de Nancy. Included were several eminent public figures: Louis de Fourcauld, Baron E. de Rothschild, Countess Sala, Princess Tenicheff, Commander Tissier, Massenet, and Richard Bouwens van der Boijen. The French state and the city of Paris provided other important commissions.

This book provides new insights into a largely undocumented period of the Gallé firm's history, from the death of its founder in 1904 to the closure of the firm in 1931. Much of the information is taken from a 1974 speech to the Montreal

Glasfax Society given by René Dézavelle, a former employee, two years before his death. Other facts on the later period were pieced together from contemporary articles made available by the Corning Museum of Glass and the Metropolitan Museum of Art. Hard business decisions had to be made by Gallé's successors – initially Dr Perdrizet, his son-in-law; then a triumvirate of all three sons-in-law, Dr Perdrizet, M. Chevalier and Professor Bourgogne – to keep the firm in existence.

During this period, the Nancy bourgeoisie still loved to astonish their tea guests with a newly acquired Gallé bibelot. But whereas small vases sold readily, larger ones – more expensively priced – did not, and these were gradually phased out. The 1925 Exposition Universelle sparked off a fresh batch of lamp and vase models. These, seen today as beautiful 1900 objects, appeared at the time dreadfully tired and outmoded. It is hard even to comprehend now why they were displayed in an exhibition of modern design. The firm's booth was rightly passed over by the international critics, ecstatic about the new technical virtuosities of Marinot and Thuret. Lalique's commercial glassware, likewise exciting, caught the period's mood.

The neighbouring Daum glassworks, which after the Great War had suffered financial vicissitudes of its own, showed that developments at the Gallé plant might have been otherwise. While the latter continued slavishly to reproduce *fin de siècle* floral glassware, by then not only *passé* but also of noticeably diminished quality, Daum adjusted its designs to the new dictates of Paris. Gallé commissions fell steadily, a decline accelerated towards 1930 when eastern France was engulfed by the World Depression. Almost all the region's glasshouses closed down, among them, at the beginning of 1931, the Gallé factory.

The illustrations in this book have been taken primarily

Above left: Gallé in his late twenties, *c.*1875;
above right: sketch of Gallé, probably 1880s;
below left: photograph of Gallé on his
exhibitor's card, Exposition Universelle, 1889;
below right: Gallé in 1900, four years before his
death

from two sources. First, Art Nouveau catalogues from
Christie's auction rooms in Geneva, New York and London.
The second source was the contemporary art magazines and
the firm's exposition catalogues (*c.*1880–1910), in which Gallé's
glassware was reviewed and pictured. A complete list of the
latter references is given in the Bibliography, together with the
major exhibitions in which they were displayed. Finally, . . .
an additional selection of sketches was kindly made available
by the Corning Museum of Glass, Dr Henry Blount and a
private European collector.

Photograph of Gallé in his atelier surrounded by plant specimens and
experimental glassware

Chapter one

Enamelling

It is sometimes supposed that Gallé let his enamelled production drop as the heady glass experimentations of the 1880s and 1890s propelled him to the new frontiers of *marqueterie de verre* and patination. This was not so. The firm continued to manufacture a wide range of crystal glassware – lemonade sets, decanters, *vide-poches*, *bonbonnières*, and toiletry items – much of which was delicately enhanced with enamelled motifs. In fact, Gallé's last exhibition, the 1904 Ecole de Nancy Exposition, included a typical selection of painted tableware – wine and champagne glasses, milk pitchers, creamers and salt-shakers. These represented a dependable source of revenue for the firm, part of the industrial production that underpinned it financially from year to year.

Gallé's initial experiments with enamelled glassware can be traced to his father's Saint-Clément faience business. Here, around 1865, Gallé *père et fils* transposed the Satsuma decoration with which they adorned their ceramics onto glass blanks. Later, liana creepers, buttercups, convolvuli and stiff-looking insects showed Gallé's awakening interest in nature. At Burgun, Schwerer & Cie in the following four years, he continued his research, familiarizing himself also with the chemical breakdown of enamels.

At the 1867 Exposition Universelle, it was evident that the technique of enamelling was back in vogue. The return to medievalism had coincided in France with the rediscovery of the Orient and, thereby, of Chinese *cloisonné*. Infatuation with the Middle Ages generated a host of decorative themes, such as Joan of Arc, heraldry and the poetry of François Villon, especially *La Ballade des dames du temps jadis*. Gallé's sources of inspiration were soon eclectic: Islamic calligraphy, Chinese Fu dogs, Japanese flora and ideograms, Greco-Roman and Bohemian glass; these and many more were given a characteristic Gallé interpretation for application onto glass.

Gallé began to experiment with his own enamels in the

early 1870s, searching for a formula to eliminate the difficulties inherent in the vitrification process. He explained the problems in a Note to the Jury of the 1884 Exposition Universelle. At too low a temperature the enamel would not adhere to the surface of the glass; at too high a temperature it would cause the vessel itself to melt. Further problems were manifest on larger pieces: the smallest change of furnace temperature would lead to blackening of the lower paintwork and insufficient fusion at the shoulder.

The design was first brushed onto the glass in a sepia-brown paint following a traditional ceramics technique (the application of enamel on to glass and pottery entails low-temperature firing known as *le petit feu*). The enamels were then applied. Sometimes the sepia outline was left as an element of decoration, at others it was overpainted in gold.

Opaque, or hard, enamels provided a powerful scale of colours. Translucent ones captured the transmitted light momentarily, providing the luminescence of church windows. Viewed in combination by reflected light, with a translucent enamel superimposed on an opaque one, the colours glowed with fierce inner brilliance.

Early enamelled examples shown at a Musée de Nancy retrospective in 1909 included a *Cornet Myosotis* (1872), a casket with a painted floral design (1875) and a pot with a monster's head (1876). In 1933, at the Pavillon de Marsan in Paris, an exhibition entitled *Le Décor de la vie sous la III République de 1870 à 1900* included another early work: a small Louis XV-style clear crystal vase painted and dated with the panorama 'Vue de St Nicolas'. Also displayed was a Louis XVI-style *bonbonnière*, engraved and gilt with a hunt scene and dated 1880. Gallé exhibited several examples at the 1884 Exposition, *De la Pierre, du bois, de la terre, et du verre*. In the same year Delaborde's long-awaited *Dictionnaire des émailleurs depuis le Moyen Age jusqu'au dix-huitième siècle* traced the medium's evolution.

Gallé used enamelling increasingly in conjunction with other forms of decoration, most commonly acid-etching, the background given either a uniform frosted finish or etched with vignettes that echoed the painted parts. At times domed glass cabochons enclosing metallic foil were applied as flower centres; at others, strips of crushed foil were sandwiched between two layers of glass. Frequently the enamelling was edged throughout in gold. Gallé reproduced a selection of these for his display in the *Histoire du verre français* Exposition in the Pavillon de l'Union Centrale at the 1900 Exposition Universelle. Pieces were inscribed *Gallé 1878–1900. Histoire du verre*.

Enamel jewels

At the 1884 Exposition, Gallé displayed what he later boldly proclaimed to be an entirely new technique: enamel jewels (*émaux-bijoux*). Successive layers of enamel were built up on a small metallic foil base, which was then fused to the surface of the glass object. In this manner, Gallé could both simulate jewelled Renaissance *objets d'art* – caskets, chalices and candlesticks – and bring the technique to bear on his modern designs. The same exhibition showed vases, trays and a bottle, all of which sparkled with imitation gemstones: enamelled emeralds, topazes, amber and rubies. Elsewhere there were 'scarabs, shards and a dragonfly with enamelled azure eyes enclosing metallic foil, its wings a diaphanous pink'.

Verre églomisé

Another traditional form of glass decoration introduced by Gallé in modernized form was *verre églomisé* in which the decoration, usually gilt or silvered, was sandwiched between two layers of glass. Gallé's technique involved the warm capsulation of *émaux-bijoux* between two layers. The resulting joint became less and less distinct in the vase's subsequent trips to the kiln as sharp edges melted into each other. Frequently, irregular pieces of crushed platinum or gold foil were also inserted. Gossamer-thin, their placement was usually random, providing an eye-catching abstract background to the main painted motifs.

Champlevé enamelling

Gallé readily acknowledged, in a self-deprecatory description of himself as a 'counterfeit stone-engraver', that he had taken the technique from sixteenth-century rock crystal *objets d'art*, one of which, *Le Coupe des Quatre Saisons*, he had seen in the Galerie d'Apollon at the Louvre. Another more immediate source of inspiration was the method of decorating copper with recessed *champs* (fields) filled with enamel.

Shallow cavities were carved or etched into the glass and then filled to the surface with low-firing translucent enamels. The holes were often first painted in gold, producing a sumptuous reflective ground for the superimposed enamels. Gallé displayed four items in 1889 to show the technique – a bowl, vase, bucket and goblet – which, in conjunction with conventional enamelling, incrustations, glass applications and metallic foil inclusions, provided infinite aesthetic variety.

Internal decoration

Superimposed layers of translucent or clear crystal supplied the ever-searching Gallé with additional means of decoration. If the surface was reserved for the vessel's primary design, then the lower layers would create secondary effects or moods by which to give the piece maximum impact.

Internal decoration had to be applied to the upper surface of the inside layer after this had been blown onto the marver and rolled flat. In some instances, powdered coloured glass or flecks of mica – which would not dissolve in fusing – were then carefully sprinkled onto its background to provide seemingly random splashes of colour or atmospheric effects such as fog, driving rain or the hazy glow of dusk. Sometimes, rods of coloured glass were converted with microsurgical precision into flower pistils. The application of a second layer sandwiched and then sealed the inclusions.

Another brilliant *intercalaire* effect, this time a borrowed technique, was achieved by injecting vapour-emitting materials into the warm paraison. These, when fused by a superimposed layer, formed elongated pockets of air which were transformed magically into raindrops or underwater aerations. The addition of manganese oxide gave the entrapped bubbles an iridescent sparkle. Although these various techniques were chemically tabulated and monitored under laboratory conditions, the hazards of the firing made it impossible to obtain two absolutely identical pieces.

At the 1884 Exposition, Gallé displayed an imitation amethyst quartz vase with air bubble inclusions and also a clear crystal cornet enclosing shredded gold and platinum metallic foil. By 1889, five years of further experimentation had brought refinement: 'Composition 81 encloses bubbles with a brownish-silver reflection that enhances the petals of a fantastic orchid.' Vase 136 included 'a vast opaque red flower (copper protoxide), with pistils and stamen enclosed in the mass; the engraver has had only to accentuate certain details in relief on the exterior of the vase.'

Chapter two

Engraving

Scarcely an item passed through the glassworks without a stop at the wheel engraver, either singly or in conjunction with Gallé's other techniques. Seated at airy, vaulted windows flanked by the tools of his trade – cutting wheels, burins, routers, chisels, and diamond styluses – the engraver had a twofold task: on the one hand, to recreate Gallé's designs within the surface of the glass, and on the other, to grind or polish away any flaws which had survived the piece's passage through the factory. He also had to give the finished glass its proud *imprimatur*: an inscribed Gallé signature.

Gallé's early essays in engraving were modelled on sixteenth- and seventeenth-century prototypes. Formal clear and tinted crystal vases and tableware were intaglio-carved with classical motifs – mythological sea monsters, stiff flower sprays and pastoral *tableaux*. The few surviving examples from the 1870s are now difficult to identify, resembling more the works of Joseph Brocard and Auguste Jean from the same period.

Several pieces from the mid-1880s show the virtuosity acquired by the firm's engravers by that time. One, a ewer-shaped crystal vase designed by Victor Prouvé and now in the Musée de l'Ecole de Nancy, is carved with angelfish and nude boys borne on the backs of snails. A second is a crystal *porte-cigares*, similarly carved with a fish and trailing seagrass beneath an enamelled and lobed rim. In both instances, the carving is microscopic in its detailing; the fish scales have a tactile quality that is startlingly life-like. Two other finely engraved pieces were displayed at the 1884 Exposition des Arts Décoratifs in Paris: the first a shell-shaped cornet decorated with classical figurines, the second the coupe *La Nuit, Le Silence, Le Sommeil*, an important early symbolist work.

In the 1889 Exposition Universelle Gallé's pieces showed a significant change. Whereas there were still a sprinkling of engraved crystal objects of traditional form – the *Orphée et Eurydice* vase was the most publicized of these – there were also numerous 'cased' or 'cameo' pieces, that is, works constructed of several layers of glass, each of a different colour, that were symbolist or naturalistic in theme and shape. Notable were *Bulbe de Lis*, *La Myrtille*, *Fruit de Véronique* and a selection of *vases de tristesse*. To Gallé's earlier transparent glassware with its random intaglio decoration had been added opaque pieces in which the *entire* surface was carved.

Gallé's technique for engraving layered, or cameo, glass was fundamentally the same as that employed in antiquity. A visit to the British Museum in 1871 had familiarized him with the Portland Vase. At the 1878 Exposition Universelle, the works of Joseph Locke and John Northwood provided further inspiration and an awareness of the technique's potential. Soon Gallé's engravers could draw infinitely more vibrancy and realism from the multicoloured mass than their predecessors had done. The glass's translucency allowed limitless gradations of colour and detailing. The sharp colour contrast in conventional cameo work was eliminated as the engraver pared away, thinning each layer to create a blended intermediate range of colours. In three-layered scenic vases, for example, a translucent red layer on top of a blue one produced the burgundy tree-line in the foreground. When the red was cut away (or etched), the remaining blue, in transparency with the yellow ground, provided the dull green of the distant trees. The blue, in turn thinned down, produced the clear turquoise of the lake and the sharp highlights of the mountain peak.

The engraver used a broad range of tools with which to work his magic. Emery, wood, cork and copper wheels of different diameter soaked in putty paste were attached to a vertical lathe and interchanged as necessary; some for work entailing a jeweller's precision, others to chisel out broad background areas or to provide the latter with a decorative *martelé* finish. Hand tools, such as burins and diamond points, were used to provide the finishing touches.

Examination of the carved cellular structure on the wings of Gallé's dragonflies or the nervate on his flower petals show them to be masterpieces of patience and manual dexterity.

Sketch by Gallé for the coupe commissioned by the Ecole Normale Supérieure as a gift to Pasteur on the occasion of his seventieth birthday (30 April 1893), displayed at the Salon Nationale des Beaux-Arts, 1893, and now in the Pasteur Museum, Paris

Chapter three

Applied and sculpted decoration

The distinction between applied and sculpted decoration is, for the purpose at hand, one of degree; the former describes the traditional form of glass application found on Gallé glassware from its beginnings until the firm's closure in 1931. The latter describes the evolution of these applications into the major free-form pieces of his last years, themselves frequently applied with organic or abstract decoration. Examples of applications on Gallé's glassware include openwork handles and the tear-shaped 'drips' which descend from the rim, either symmetrically or at random, on several of his tableware services. Domed or prismatic glass cabochons provided an alternative form of decoration, their carved or painted surfaces catching the sun's brilliance as the viewer moved around the room.

Until the late 1890s, Gallé depended more on elaborate openwork mounts than on applications of glass to enhance the formal shape of his glassware. A sketch in an article by Louis de Fourcaud in *La Revue d'art ancien et moderne* (1898), however, marked the transition now imminent: five crystal vessels were conceived as spiralling arum lilies rising from bulbous bases. It was no longer necessary to apply floral or marine decoration to a vase of conventional baluster, trumpet or cylindrical shape. Now the vase itself would be fashioned into a flower or wave. Seen in retrospect, this was the inevitable fusion of Gallé's dual passion for glass and nature. The long-standing alliance now merged: the theme became the object, and vice versa.

The technique required great virtuosity and patience on the part of the glassblower; numerous trips to the kiln were needed as the heating and modelling process repeated itself. Free-form vases were themselves applied with free-form decoration. *La Feuille de Rhubarbe* and *La Feuille Rongée* coupes provided powerful examples: to the body's organic form were added entwined trailing leafage and tendrils, each individually shaped on the marver and added warm to the heated body so that the two would fuse and anneal. An item was assembled piecemeal, each motif shaped with pincers and scissors before application. Pistils and stamen, exquisitely rendered, were imbedded with microsurgical precision into flower centres. Elsewhere, a rhinoceros beetle, sculpted in full relief, became the dominant motif on a vase depicting the undergrowth of a Javanese forest.

The 1900 Exposition Universelle came just too soon for Gallé's sculpted flora to have reached the peak of their perfection. Included, however, were two vases which are today considered masterpieces: *Le Lys* and *L'Orchidée*. The former showed the technique at its most sophisticated, being modelled as a red water lily corolla encompassed by a languid lily spray with trailing luminous white bud and blossom. *L'Orchidée* is seen, by comparison, as a somewhat less successful, transitional piece, its double-lozenge-shaped body too stiff to portray the haunting symbolism of the live and dead orchids carved on its front and back. Also shown at the 1900 Exposition were *La Violette*, *La Solanée*, *Flambé d'Eau*, and *Iris et Libellule*, all with applied and sculpted decoration of varying complexity.

The best was yet to come. Sometime in the 1901–02 period, Gallé introduced *La Main*, a piece which demands, in its forceful but enigmatic symbolism, to be considered as the master's *chef d'oeuvre*. Curiously, no reference appears to have been made to it by Gallé or by any contemporary critic, leaving open the issue of when it was made, and for whom. On reflection, its macabre subject matter indicates that it was more likely the product of the master's private surrealist probings than a commissioned piece. It remains a tantalizing enigma, raising more questions than it can answer.

The following year came *Les Roses de France* and *Le Chêne*. In 1903, there was a fresh harvest of new pieces at the Pavillon de Marsan in Paris, many of major importance: *La Hippocampe*, *La Feuille de Rhubarbe*, *Fôret Javanaise*, *La Feuille Rongée*, *L'Orge*, *L'Eucalyptus*, *La Libellule*, and the Pine Cone vase. In 1904, the year of his death, Gallé created a fitting capstone to his career: the magnificent *Les Coprins* mushroom table lamp commissioned by his friend and great patron, the magistrate Henri Hirsch.

Two points should be made here concerning the manufacture of such works. First, almost none of these major models was unique, as is sometimes presumed. Successful designs were executed in series of four or five, the detail varying slightly in line with the artistic interpretation and manual dexterity of the glass artisan. Very few *pièces uniques* were commissioned; even *Les Coprins* and *La Main* were produced *en série*. Close examination of contemporary literature shows that a vase which, at first glance, appears to have been illustrated in different publications, is, in fact, three or four variations of the same model. *L'Orchidée* provides a good example: first displayed at the 1900 Exposition Universelle, it was reproduced at least three times within two years, after which other reproductions followed.

The second point is that Gallé almost certainly did not himself execute any of these works. Preoccupied with the administration of a furniture, ceramic and glass factory, and the responsibility of generating business, he could at best probably only sketch the preliminary designs and oversee various stages of their creation. A small, but highly talented and long-serving, team of glassblowers and engravers translated his ideas into glass. Nor did production of major works summarily cease on Gallé's death. Several were produced posthumously. An example is the *Lys* vase now in the Conservatoire National des Arts et Métiers in Paris. A contemporary magazine lists its year of manufacture and exhibition at the Champ-de-Mars salon as 1906. The date coincides with the Conservatory's accession records.

Chapter four

Marqueterie de verre

Gallé filed his patent for *marqueterie de verres ou cristaux* on 26 April 1898. Singly, the technique represented the height of his achievements in glass; in conjunction with his other processes it offered unlimited aesthetic possibilities. As a critic in *La Lorraine illustrée* wrote: 'The process presents the glassmaker with a great intellectual challenge . . . transforming him into an artist, decorator, colourist, and landscapist.'

The fundamentals of the technique were known to the glassblowers of antiquity, who had inserted glass cones and beads into the vitreous mass of glass as decoration. Later, Venetian glasshouses popularized the use of millefiori insertions. In the mid-nineteenth century, St Louis, Baccarat and Clichy presented their paperweights to an astonished world: miniature objects of vertu in which glass flowers and reptiles were encased in crystal with bewildering complexity. Gallé took the technique even further, stretching it to the medium's practical limits.

In a 1905 article in *L'Art décoratif*, Jules Henrivaux described *marqueterie de verre* as 'the adaption to glass of the art applied to wood'. The two were distinctly similar. Pieces of coloured glass, cut to a predetermined form, were imbedded with pincers in the paraison. This was rolled flat on the marver until the insertions were flush with its surface. Shaped and annealed, the newly formed vase was ready for its next stage, usually a trip to the engraver's wheel or, on occasion, encasement in a clear layer in the technique common to paperweights.

If the principle, as Henrivaux wrote, was simple, its execution was not. The coefficients of expansion of each inset coloured piece of glass were different, a problem compounded by the fact that they were themselves often made up of two or more laminated layers. The glassblower had to select colours which would expand and contract at the same speed, thereby minimizing the possibility of cracking during the multiple reheatings and coolings necessary as every piece – often more than ten – was inserted. On completion, the engraver would provide the inlaid piece of glass – flowers or marine life – with its necessary detail. Laminated pieces had their top layer pared away to provide a strikingly realistic bi-coloured effect.

Examples of Gallé's early *marqueterie de verre* on crystal were illustrated in *Art et décoration* in 1898. These, entitled 'Les Safrans d'Hiver', consisted of vases adorned with a popular theme – red, amber and mauve crocuses on tall swaying stems.

The 1900 Exposition Universelle provided Gallé with the showpiece necessary to present his new techniques to an adoring public. Numerous colourful pieces bear mention: *Chardon des Alpes*, *Colchique* and *Iris et Libellule*. By 1902 the process was further refined; the series of dragonfly coupes was introduced, as was the important bronze-mounted *Chêne* vase and the *Roses de France*. During this period a selection of marquetry pieces was acquired by the Hamburg Museum, others by the Luxembourg Museum, and others, again, by the Musée des Arts Décoratifs in Paris. In 1914, the auction of Roger Marx's collection included other important examples: *Les Anemones*, *La Solanée*, *La Violette* and *Les Joyaux de la Mer*.

The constant heating and cooling cycle created innumerable stress factors within the glass so that a considerable number of marquetry pieces cracked prior to completion. Some were early essays, tentative steps on the road to mastery of the new technique; others, later examples, flawed possibly in their last firing. Even so, many of these were deemed to be *chef d'oeuvres* worthy of retention, despite their incompletion or impairment. Such pieces were inscribed 'Etude'. The absence of this identification on a cracked piece indicates that the damage was incurred after it left the factory.

Sometimes individual inlaid pieces of glass on a marquetry vase are seen under close inspection to contain on their perimeter several hairline cracks. These are frequently almost indiscernible: minute separations or 'flashes' that occurred in the cooling process. To a collector, these should not in themselves constitute damage.

'Etude' pieces are always of academic interest, being often of high quality and beauty. They can be compared to Tiffany's Favrile 'Lava' glassware which suffered a similarly high casualty rate due to the excessive kiln temperatures required. Tiffany, like Gallé, is reputed to have set the most rigid standards of quality control. Stories abound of pieces summarily smashed with a walking stick as, ever-vigilant, he made his rounds of the Corona works in later years. Invoices from Tiffany Studios show, however, that 'Lava' pieces *were* sold in damaged condition; several items are listed with 'internal cracks'. Clearly, both Gallé and Tiffany realized that the probability of perfection in their most prized techniques was sufficiently low for them to bend otherwise rigid standards.

Patination

Combustion furnaces – coke- or wood-burning – emit particles of chemical dust and vapour into the atmosphere. Inevitably, some of these are deposited on the piece of glass under fabrication, giving its surface variously a matt, cloudy or slightly corroded texture. This effect has always been considered a negative by-product of the glassmaking process, to be contained to the maximum extent possible. Characteristically, Gallé decided that if he could not control the process to the point of full elimination, he would harness it positively in the pursuit of beauty.

Jules Henrivaux described Gallé's technique of patination in *L'Art décoratif* as a form of devitrification which obtained 'the textured effects of textiles, leather, snow and rain . . . which one can then crackle, flute, speckle, engrave and decorate . . .' Gallé learnt to master the effect – to the extent that it was fully controllable at all – through many years of research. His Note to the Jury of the 1889 Exposition Universelle refers to recent experimentation with *patine du verre*. Later, several patinated pieces were shown at the 1892 salon of the Champ-de-Mars. In 1897 Gallé finally applied for a patent, presenting at the same time the application for his *marqueterie de verre*.

The impurities were now trapped and stored in advance, to be used when and as required either by being rolled directly onto the paraison or by being blown into the furnace. The effect, as Henri Frantz wrote in the *Studio*, was governed by the complex interaction of chemicals, furnace temperatures and length of firing.

His mastery of patination allowed Gallé to pursue nature's passing moods: the burgeoning of spring or dawn's evanescent mists. Effects included storminess, underwater currents and murkiness, and patterning on leaves. More complex effects were achieved in layered glass. As Gallé explained:

> Patination can occur under a layer of crystal if the piece is blown, the bed of dust becoming imprisoned and compressed between two layers of glass. Unable to escape, the gas remaining from the original combustion presses against the glass paste and forms bubbles that lodge near the centre of the mass. In this patina one can make decorative reserves, either by protecting them while still hot or, once cold, by cutting into the patinated ground . . . providing an infinite variety of design possibilities.

A small marine vase at the 1900 Exposition Universelle, entitled *La Patine des Verres*, showed another popular effect: the surface of the trailing seaweed was speckled with iridescence, depicting the oily slime that forms in stagnant pools.

Patination was used in conjunction with all Gallé's techniques, in particular *marqueterie de verre*, with which it proved especially effective.

Chapter five

Verreries parlantes

Gallé drew widely on literature as an inspiration for his creations in glass and wood. Numerous quotations appear on his furniture and glassware; the former branded or in marquetry, the latter carved, etched or enamelled, and referred to by Gallé as *verreries parlantes* (literally 'speaking glassware'). Verses on glass became *poèmes vitrifiés*.

One of the earliest known examples is a brushholder, shown at the 1884 Exposition Universelle and now in the Musée de l'Ecole de Nancy, which bears an inscription from François Villon's *La Ballade des dames du temps jadis*. The legend is carved in relief in a medieval cursive script: 'La Reyne Blanche comme un lys, qui chantait à voix de Sirène.' Other examples show the same preoccupation with detail in their chosen calligraphy.

Sometimes a single line was drawn from a poem to underline the vase's theme; sometimes a couplet or stanza. The poet's name invariably followed. If the quotation was Gallé's own, it remained unattributed. Several inscribed vases were probably conceived in reverse: the naturalism or symbolism evoked within the glass reminded Gallé of a relevant quotation, requiring that the piece make a final journey to the engraver for its post-inscription.

The range of quotations on Gallé's glassware pays tribute to his voracious appetite for reading. It is impossible to cite all the influences: the vast majority were poets and playwrights, others men-of-letters drawn, seemingly at random, from history. Symbolists took pride of place: Baudelaire, Montesquiou, Hugo and Maeterlinck. Others included Dante, Shakespeare, Virgil, Hesiod, St Francis of Assisi, Gautier, Leconte de Lisle, Prudhomme, Chateaubriand, de Musset and Lamartine. The list passes to lesser-knowns . . . Rodenbach, Guérin, Dupont, Hinzelin . . . and still it appears endless. One begins to comprehend the extent of Gallé's intellect in his ability to retain and draw on such a range of references.

Gallé's poetic sentiments were of more than intellectual inspiration. There was also, as he wrote in his Note to the Jury of the 1884 Exposition Universelle, an unpredictable technical benefit:

> The very process of research may summon up deep-lying memories, and these in turn prompt further technical research and attempts to utilize them in art . . . the wish to recreate on pottery such themes as the legends of Lorraine, the shepherdess of Domremy or the King of Jerusalem's miraculous hunt has inspired the search for enamels in soft colours . . .

Chapter six

Imitation hardstones and agates

At the 1884 Exposition Universelle, Gallé introduced his imitation hardstone glassware. His Note to the Jury proclaimed boldly a host of technical innovations: startling colourations and simulated effects had been achieved by the introduction of metallic oxides and salts into the vitreous glass mass. Jade, agate, jasper, onyx, quartz, even precious stones such as sapphires, emeralds and amethysts, emerged from the furnace as if hewn from quarried rock. The deep honey-gold tones and granulations of amber, a fossil resin born of water, were reproduced with close fidelity.

By 1889 the range of effects was manifold: subtle infusions of iron or chrome oxides, cobalt and manganese, produced smokiness, speckling, marbling and dichroism. Iridium and thallium, prohibitively expensive for commercial production, were used on commissioned pieces to bring shadings to opaque colours. Combinations of oxides allowed Gallé 'an infinite variety of accidents and nuances completely untried in the art of glassmaking'.

A critic summed up Gallé's achievements in a 1903 article in the *Studio*:

He studied the science of colouring with fresh ardour; and whereas he had hitherto relied mainly upon the vegetable kingdom for his decorative inspirations, he now determined to make the sister realm of minerals yield up her secrets of subtle colouring. By mixing ordinary white glass, before it cooled in the crucible preparations, with a metallic base and pulverised glass, M. Gallé managed to vary infinitely the delicate shades of colouring and the degrees of transparency of his vases, giving to them some of the qualities of precious stones. In them will be found now the opalescent greens of the chrysoberyl or of the chrysolite, the silvery gleam of the cymophane, the scarlet glow of the cinnamonstone, the blue of the turquoise, and all the variegated shades of the amethyst – in a word, the artist rings the changes on the complete scale of Nature's colours. Sunstones and moonstones, milky opals, agates with mystic markings, variegated quartzes and granites, garnets and sardonyx, one and all have been compelled in their turn to yield up the most jealously hidden secrets of Nature's own transmuting furnace, in the crucibles of the master-magician of the glass-manufactory in Nancy.

The technique of 'crackling' (*craquelure*) was borrowed from François Rousseau and his disciple, Ernest Léveillé. Gallé wrote in 1889: 'I have reproduced the glistening fissures in certain quartzes by throwing cold water onto the vase during its creation.'

Chapter seven

Verres hyalites and vases de tristesse

The 1889 Exposition Universelle saw the introduction of Gallé's *verres hyalites*, also called *vases noirs*. Included were vases inspired by what he described as 'quite sad aspects'. The best known of these is *Orphée et Eurydice*, designed by Victor Prouvé to portray the moment when the imprudent Greek hero turned to view his wife on their way back from Hades. The engraved vision of the tragic lovers receives dramatic impact in the black-streaked, bubbled glass which swirls upward to the surface. Elsewhere, *L'Amour Chassant les Papillons Noirs* shows an eager cupid pursuing black butterflies, an allegory on the elusiveness of love. Another vase depicts a swarm of moths escaping upward, symbolizing souls departing from the bodies of the dead.

Gallé's Note to the Jury suggests that the themes of these early hyalite vases evolved from his success in creating black glass, rather than the reverse. The technique was discussed at length: 'The grey glint which gives a sort of iridescence to this material comes from the reduction of iron peroxide in the coal-filled air of the lading-hole of the furnace during the work.' Little reference was made to their haunting subject matter, the inhabitants of our nightmares.

Three years later, however, at the Champ-de-Mars, it was the message rather than the medium that took prominence. Renamed more appropriately *vases de tristesse*, the theme was sharply pronounced: death, decay and the ephemeral aspect of life. Gallé revealed his existential doubts in a small section of vases exhibited amid a wondrous display of multicoloured glassware that trumpeted his miraculous new technical feats. Black still predominated, now on pale, translucent or clear grounds heightened with traces of amethyst or opal. Emphasized were carnivorous insects and plants; creatures of the night; and the sadness of autumn, winter's foreboding.

Another frequent theme was the ocean bed, in the late 1800s still a murky unknown. Gallé designed black marine vases until his death, most depicting the Maris-Stella species of seagrass among mollusks and starfish. In 1903, he exhibited another well-known model, *Les Feuilles des Douleurs Passées*.

Roger Marx provided a most eloquent assessment of the *vases de tristesse* in his 1905 lecture on Gallé at the Academie de Stanislas, published in the *Bulletin des Sociétés Artistiques de l'Est*:

On the surface of glass which has the waxen dullness of a great candle, half-faded flowers exhale the ephemeral and sorrow-filled 'beauty of mortal things', and, in its lament for Ariel, the crystal will don mourning weeds of fog, or clouds crossed by the shadow of a flight of bats. The melancholy of autumn will be evoked by colchicums and bilberries whose leaves are splotched with stains like ghostly chrysanthemums, and wild ranunculus bowed over in the mist. Winter, winter, too is recalled with its inclemency, harshness and frosts. Here is a procession of frozen little birds whose tracks stretch out in the snow. Here are alpine soldanelles eager for air and sun. Here are plants asleep beneath the frost, like a poet's happiness.

'For the sadness of my joy
is like grass under the ice.'
(M. Maeterlinck)

Chapter eight

Mounts

Gallé used mounts sparingly on his glassware, preferring that a piece be freestanding or rest on an applied glass foot. Early examples (c.1885) show the eighteenth-century influence which was still strong on glassmakers and ceramicists of the late 1800s: Louis XV- and XVI-style gilt-bronze socles with pierced latticework and foliate decoration provided a decorative fillip to vessels engraved or painted with classical themes. Gallé's later mounts show that in time he came to view them as an integral part of the total composition. In one mount, trailing bronze seaweed spirals upward to encircle a marine vase, terminating in crested waves that cover its freeform mouth. In another, a slender leaf emerges from a bed of tangled foliage to follow the contours of the cylindrical glass stem of a table lamp base, providing both structural support and increased naturalistic effect.

With few exceptions, Gallé produced the wood, bronze and wrought-iron mounts in his own workshops. Wood models were sculpted in the furniture department under the supervision of Emile Lang. Paul Holderbach and Edouard Dignon were listed in 1903 as specifically responsible for their creation. Due to the intrinsic bulkiness and inflexibility of the material, wood mounts were of simple, if not formal, design, often of flaring square or hexagonal form carved with berries and overlapping leaves. At the 1892 salon at the Champ-de-Mars, Gallé displayed a range of glassware mounted on wood bases, including a table lamp comprised of a carved glass corolla shade on an oak foot; a *Secrets de la Mer* scent bottle on a small ebony socle elaborately carved with seaweed, crabs and mollusks; and a *Flore Fossile* vase on a *gayac* base sculpted as an inverted pine cone.

However, bronze and wrought-iron mounts were much preferred because of their durability and visual lightness. These were made in the same small metalwork shop and foundry in which the furniture mounts were cast. Messrs Heck and Roth

were listed in 1904 as the firm's metal mount specialists. Bronze dragonflies and bats, frozen in flight, were assigned either to support glass incense burners or to adorn the frieze drawers and key plates on marquetry desks.

Several important glass commissions incorporated intricate bronze mounts, some of which were themselves adorned with incrusted glass jewels; in the 1890s, the *Cattleya* vase offered to the Empress of Russia and a cornet inspired by a Victor Hugo verse, 'L'étoile du matin, l'étoile du soir'. In 1903 several Exposition pieces were similarly enhanced: *Le Chêne, Le Lierre, Urne Agate* and *Gourde aux Ephémères*. Wrought-iron was generally preferred to bronze for oversized objects, such as two monumental amphora vases – one, commissioned for the wedding of M. Eugène Corbin, is now in the Musée de l'Ecole de Nancy; the other, inspired by King Solomon, was sold at auction in Paris in 1981.

A royal, state or private commission sometimes justified a mount made of precious metal. For these Gallé turned to the foremost gold- and silversmiths of the day. None appears to have been especially favoured; the skills of Cardeilhac, Lucien Falize, Froment-Meurice, Gerard Sandoz, Bonvallet and *L'Escalier de Cristal* were all called upon, while Fabergé provided the silver floral mount for a vase presented to the Russian Grand-Duke Sergé in the mid-1890s. A 1902 article by Maurice Demaison in *Art et décoration* shows several fine examples of mounted Gallé bases.

Mounts manufactured by the Gallé factory are frequently unsigned, whereas commissioned ones usually bear the inscribed name or impressed hallmarks of the gold- or silversmith. *L'Escalier de Cristal*, a retail firm directed at the turn of the century by the Pannier brothers, provided numerous mounts for the glassware which Gallé offered through their retail shop at 1 rue Aubert, Paris.

Les Secrets de la Mer, applied and engraved bottle on a sculpted ebony base, inspired by a verse from Baudelaire

'O Mer, nul ne connait tes richesses intones,
  Homme, nul n'a sonde le fond de tes abîmes,
  Tant vous êtes jaloux de garder vos secrets'
displayed at the Champ-de-Mars, Paris, 1892

Plates 1–4
Glass techniques used in
conjunction

1
Glass techniques used in conjunction:
(*a*) engraving; (*b*) etching and wheel-
polishing; (*c*) *marqueterie de verre* and
engraving; (*d*) mould-blowing and
etching; (*e*) *marqueterie de verre* and
engraving★

a   b   c   d   e

2
Glass techniques used in conjunction:
(*a*) engraving and enamelling;
(*b*) mould-blowing, etching and
wheel-polishing; (*c*) engraving;
(*d*) *marqueterie de verre*, engraving
and *verre parlant* inscription
'Commencer sur la terre et vivre
dans les cieux Méry'; (*e*) marquetry
with bronze mount

★*see page 14 for explanation
of illustration sources*

a   b   c   d   e

3
Glassware showing various Gallé techniques:
(*a*) engraving and internal decoration;
(*b*) etching; (*c*) enamelling and etching;
(*d*) enamelling, engraving and application;
(*e*) *marqueterie de verre* and engraving

4
Glassware from Roger Marx's collection, auctioned in Paris in 1914:
(*a*) *La Solanée*, applied and marquetry flaçon, 11¾in (30cm) high, *c.*1900;
(*b*) *Les Algues*, engraved and applied flaçon, 9¾in (25cm) high, *c.*1900;
(*c*) *Le Cyclamen*, marquetry and engraved vase, 7in (18cm) high, *c.*1900;
(*d*) *L'Ail*, applied vase, 12½in (32cm) high, *c.*1900;
(*e*) *La Pervenche*, marquetry and engraved vase, inscribed 'Pervincio', 4¼in (11cm) high, *c.*1900;
(*f*) *De Tout mon Coeur*, marquetry and engraved vase, inscribed 'De Tout Mon Coeur', 13¾in (35cm) high, *c.*1895
(*g*) *La Violette*, marquetry and applied coupe, 9¾in (25cm) high, *c.*1900;
(*h*) *L'Orge*, engraved 4-layered cameo vase, 13in (33cm) high, *c.*1902

a   b   c   d   e

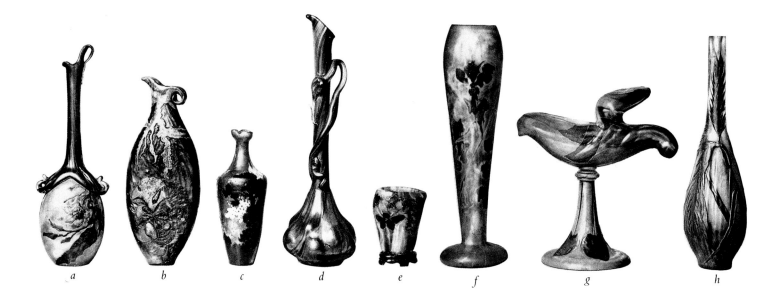

a   b   c   d   e   f   g   h

Plates 5–46:
Enamelled glassware

5
Enamelled claret service, comprising a carafe,
tumblers and a tray

6
Enamelled liqueur service, comprising a
decanter, tray and 12 liqueurs

7
Enamelled glassware: (*a*) *clair-de-lune* bottle, 7in (18cm) high; (*b*) decanter, 7 liqueurs and stand, 8in (20cm) height of decanter

8
Enamelled pitcher and beer glasses

9
Enamelled, applied and engraved pitcher,
7¾in (19cm) high

10
Enamelled vase, 7¼in (18.5cm) high

11
Enamelled and etched vase, 8¼in (20.5cm) high

12
Enamelled and etched vase, 11⅞in (30cm) high

13
Enamelled and etched bottle, 8in (20cm) high

14
Enamelled glassware: double vase, 9¼in
(23.5cm) high; and ewer, 10¼in (26cm) high

15
Enamelled and engraved vase, modelled as a
Fu dog, 5¼in (13.5cm) high

16
Four enamelled vases

17
Four enamelled vases

18
Enamelled glassware

19
Enamelled and etched glassware

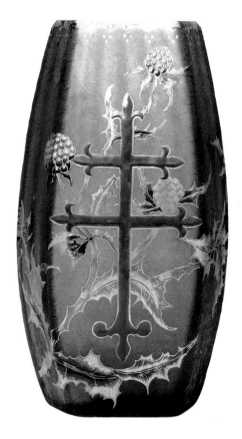

20
Enamelled and etched *verre parlant* vase inscribed 'Exposition 1878 Redité en sa Cristallerie pour l'histoire du verre Gallé 1900', 10¾in (27cm) high

21
Enamelled and etched vase, 10in (25.5cm) high

22
Enamelled and engraved glassware

23
Enamelled, etched and applied covered dish,
8in (20cm) diameter

24
Enamelled, engraved and applied glassware

25
Enamelled crystal tableware, *c.*1904

28
Selection of enamelled crystal tableware,
Ecole de Nancy Exposition, Paris, 1903

29
Enamelled *verre parlant* and applied vase
inscribed 'Moy archevesque et duc de Reins
suis tenu par divin moi en de oindre le roy
tres cretien' and 'Moy premier per Duc de
Bourcogne doy aller au sacre du Roy pour
porter sa courone en noble erroy', 7¾in
(19.6cm) high

30
Enamelled and applied carp vase, 11⅛in
(28.3cm) high

31
Selection of enamelled and applied glassware
including a ewer, bowl (*La Source*), and two
Baptismal vases, one offered to Princess
Marguerite of Chartres, Duchess of Magenta,
on the occasion of her marriage, displayed at
the Salon Nationale des Beaux-Arts, Paris,
1897

32
Enamelled and engraved glassware, the circular ashtray inscribed 'Fumer est plaisir – plaisir est fumée'

33
Enamelled glassware, the central goblet inscribed 'La Royne blanche comme ung Lys qui chantait à voy de Sirène' and dated 1884 and 1900

34, 35
Two enamelled 13-piece liqueur services

36
Enamelled vase, 14⅝in (37cm) high

37
Enamelled vase, 9¼in (23.5cm) high

38
Pair of enamelled vases, 9in (23cm) high

39
Enamelled and applied *clair-de-lune* and *verre parlant* bottle with stopper, inscribed 'L'office du soir à la distillerie' and 'Prions nous pauvre père Gaucher qui sacrifie son âme aux intérêts de la communauté, Alphonse Daudet', 11⅛in (28.3cm) high

40
Enamelled and applied vase, 15in (38cm) high

41
Two enamelled vases: 8¼in (21cm) high; and 14¼in (36cm) high

44
Enamelled and etched coffret, 5½in (14cm) high

45
Enamelled vase, 9in (23cm)

46
Selection from enamelled 106-piece stemware service comprising 8 liqueurs, 20 sherries, 14 clarets, 20 hocks, 11 champagnes, 18 water glasses, 2 plates, 2 covered bowls, 2 handled *bonbonnières* and 9 decanters

Plates 47–89:
Engraved glassware

47
L'Orée des Bois, engraved vase, Ecole de
Nancy Exposition, Paris, 1903

48
Oceano Nox, engraved marine bowl, Ecole de
Nancy Exposition, Paris, 1903

49
Premier Gel d'Automne, engraved vase, Ecole
de Nancy Exposition, Paris, 1903

50
L'Eruption, engraved vase, Ecole de Nancy
Exposition, Paris, 1903

51
Maris-Stella, engraved marine vase, Ecole de
Nancy Exposition, Paris, 1903

52
Two engraved vases: $6\frac{1}{4}$in (16cm) high; and $12\frac{1}{4}$in (31cm) high

53
Engraved and applied glassware: (*a*) bottle with stopper, $6\frac{1}{4}$in (16cm) high; (*b*) vase, $4\frac{1}{4}$in (11.5cm) high; (*c*) vase, $5\frac{7}{8}$in (15cm) high

a   *b*   *c*

54
Engraved glassware: magnolia ewer, previously in the collection of Gustav V of Sweden, $9\frac{3}{4}$in (25cm) high; and marquetry vase decorated with a hemerocallis (day lily), $12\frac{1}{4}$in (31cm) high

55
Engraved vases: (*a*) $4\frac{3}{4}$in (12cm) high; (*b*) $7\frac{7}{8}$in (20cm) high; (*c*) $5\frac{3}{4}$in (14.5cm) high

a   *b*   *c*

56
Le Lis Marin, engraved marine vase, Ecole de
Nancy Exposition, Paris, 1903

57
Les Ciselures de la Mer, two engraved vases,
Ecole de Nancy Exposition, Paris, 1903

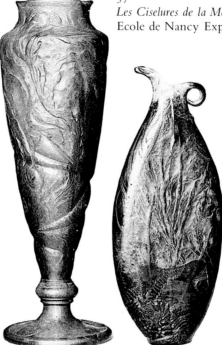

58
Engraved ewer-shaped vase with angelfish,
designed by Victor Prouvé, 10½in (27cm)
high, displayed at the 1884 Exposition
Universelle and now in the Musée de l'Ecole
de Nancy

59
Engraved *solifleur* vase inscribed 'Seulette suis
seulette veux être' and 'fait par l'amant des
frissonnantes libellules', Exposition
Universelle, Paris, 1889

60
Engraved vase, 8in (20.5cm) high

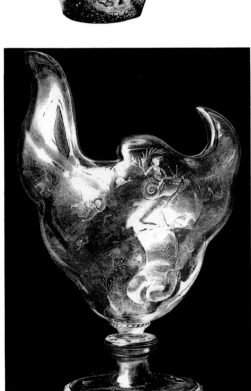

61
Begonia de Lemoine, engraved vase, Exposition
Universelle, Paris, 1900

62
Clématite de Lemoine, engraved vase,
Exposition Universelle, Paris, 1900

63
Sketch of two vases, *c.*1900, showing (*a*) *La
Solanée*

a

64
Engraved coupe, seal and marine vase, Salon
Nationale des Beaux-Arts, Paris, 1904

65
Vases in which engraving is
incorporated with other
techniques

67
Engraved brush holder, 3⅛in (8cm) high

68
Engraving incorporated with other techniques: (*a*) corolla table lamp, 13in (33cm) high; (*b*) *verre parlant* vase inscribed 'La Myrtille des Bois', 6¾in (17cm) high; (*c*) marquetry and *verre parlant* vase inscribed 'Dans le ciel des ailes, des ailes – Pierre Guillard'

a *b* *c*

69
Engraved vase, Exposition Lorraine de la
Société des Amis des Arts, Nancy, 1904

70
Engraved bowl with moths, Salon Nationale
des Beaux-Arts, Paris, 1905

71
Engraved and enamelled compote, 5¼in
(13.5cm) high

72
Engraved and enamelled crystal vase,
displayed at the Exposition Universelle, Paris,
1889, now in the Musée des Arts Décoratifs,
Paris

73
Engraved glassware, Salon Nationale des
Beaux-Arts, Paris, 1904

74
Two engraved vases, Salon Nationale des
Beaux-Arts, Paris, 1905, including
(a) *L'Orge*, ex Roger Marx collection

a

75
Five-layered cameo vase, etched and
engraved, Exposition Universelle, 1889

76
Le Sommeil des Coccinelles, engraved vase with
applied cabochons, 9½in (24cm) high,
ex Roger Marx collection

77
Engraved Exposition vase inscribed
'Exposition 1889', 3¼in (8.5cm) high

78, 79
Engraved and etched glassware

80
Porte-rose vase in smoky quartz glass, displayed
at the Exposition Universelle, 1889

81
Les Carnivores, engraved 5-layered vase,
collection of Mme Paul Lenglet, Exposition
Universelle, 1889

82
Engraved crystal decanter and stemware,
1890s

83
Three vases engraved with classical themes,
Exposition Universelle, 1889

84
*La Cri Strident de Mon Désir – Comte de
Noailles*, engraved crystal vase with fitted case,
1890s

85
Engraved, marquetry and applied chalice,
1890s

86
Engraved and *intercalaire* bottle with stopper,
8¾in (22.2cm) high

87
Vase in engraved crystal, Exposition
Universelle, 1889

88
Sketch of lily-shaped engraved crystal
glassware, *c.*1897

89
Engraved glassware exhibited at the Exposition Universelle, 1889:
shell-shaped vase, collection of M. Edouard Corroyer; and coupe
entitled *La Nuit, Le Silence, Le Sommeil,*
collection of M. Ramon de Errazu

Plates 90–126:
Applied glassware

90
Applied, marquetry and *intercalaire* pine cone
vase, 17in (43.2cm) high

91
La Feuille de Rhubarbe, applied, marquetry and
patinated coupe, 12⅜in (31.5cm) long

92
Le Lis à Longues Fleurs, applied vase,
Exposition Universelle, Paris, 1900

93
Applied cameo ewer, 10¾in (27.5cm) high

94
Applied and engraved bowl, 6½in (16.5cm)
high

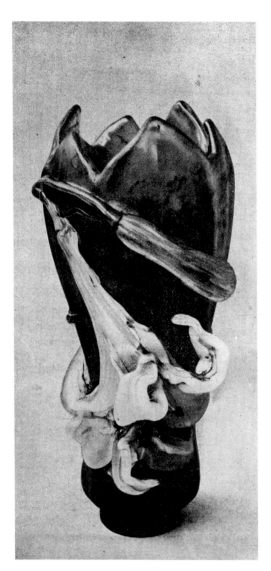

95
Applied and marquetry
vase, 1904

96
Roses de France, applied and marquetry vase,
1902

97
Herbier Maritime, applied and marquetry vase,
Salon Nationale des Beaux-Arts, Paris, 1904

98
L'Orchidée, applied and *intercalaire* vase (model also known as *fleur de glace*), 9⅞in (22.5cm) high

99
La Feuille de Chou, applied coupe, 5⅞in (15cm) high

100
Applied and engraved vase, 10in (25cm) high

101
Applied and engraved marine vase, 13½in
(34cm) high

Butterfly vase with applied cabochons,
Exposition Universelle, 1889, now in the
Conservatoire des Arts et Métiers, Paris

Le Lys, applied vase, 1906, now in the
Conservatoire des Arts et Métiers, Paris

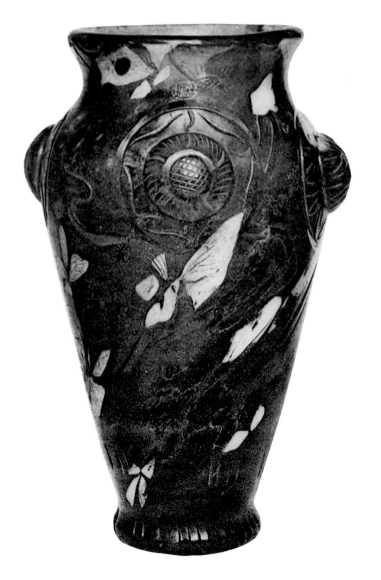

104, 105
Two applied and engraved vases, Exposition
Universelle, 1900

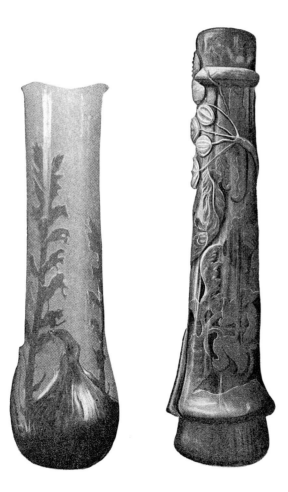

106
A Victor Prouvé, ses Amis, applied presentation
vase, 1896

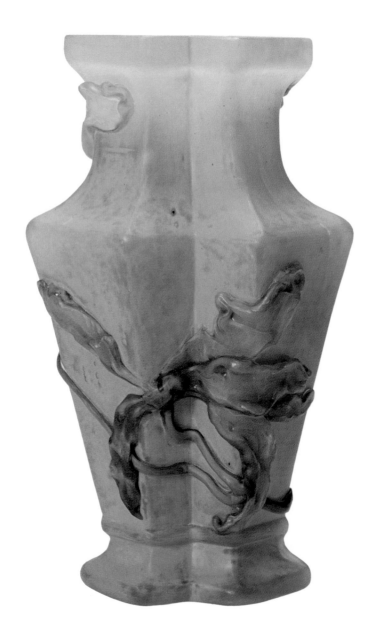

107
L'Orchidée, applied and engraved vase, 9in
(23cm) high

108
La Libellule, applied and marquetry coupe,
7½in (19cm) high, 8in (20.5cm) diameter

109
Le Hippocampe, applied and engraved vase, displayed at the Ecole de Nancy Exposition, Paris, 1903

110
Applied and marquetry glassware: a covered chalice; and a *solifleur* vase

111
Le Lys, applied vase, Salon Nationale des Beaux-Arts, Paris, 1905

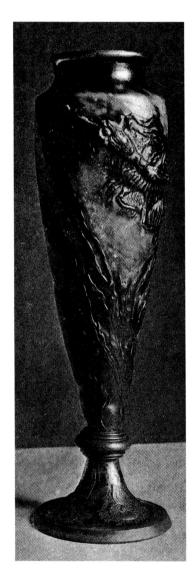

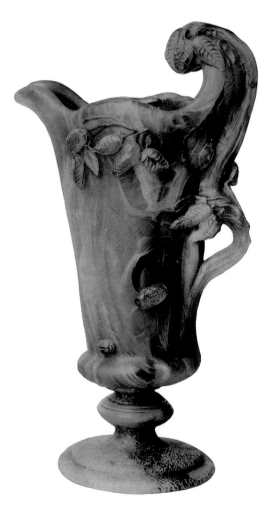

112
Applied and marquetry coupe, Salon
Nationale des Beaux-Arts, Paris, 1905

113
Two applied and marquetry vases, c.1904

114
La Fleur de Gentiane, applied and *intercalaire* vase, inscribed '1889', 8¼in (21.5cm) high

115
Applied and engraved *intercalaire* bottle, 7½in
(19cm) high

116
La Feuille Rongée, applied marine vase,
displayed at the Ecole de Nancy Exposition,
Paris, 1903

117
Applied and engraved marine vase, *c.*1902

118
L'Eucalyptus, applied and marquetry vase,
displayed at the Ecole de Nancy Exposition,
Paris, 1903

119
Chevaux de Mer, applied vase, displayed at the
Ecole de Nancy Exposition, Paris, 1903

120
Lilium Longiflorum, applied and engraved
bronze-mounted vase, displayed at the Ecole
de Nancy Exposition, Paris, 1903

121
Forêt Javanaise, applied and marquetry vase,
displayed at the Ecole de Nancy Exposition,
Paris, 1903

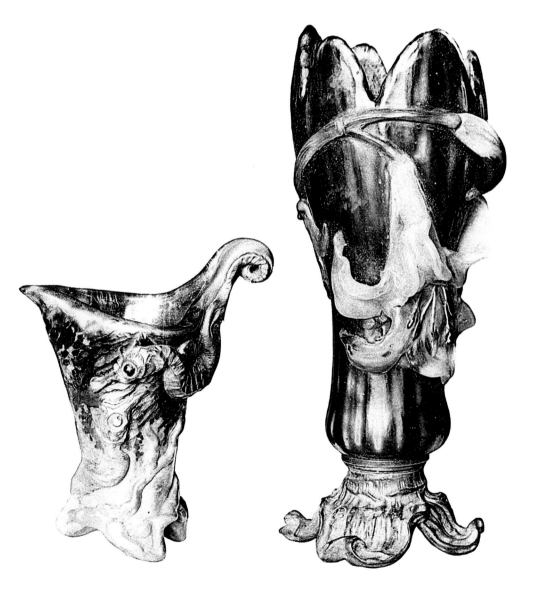
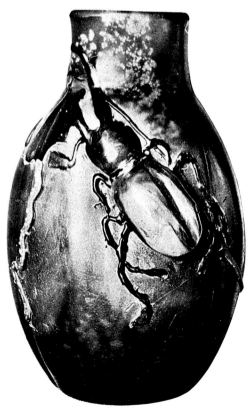

123
Roses de France, applied and engraved vase,
7½in (19cm) high

124
Ephémère Rose, applied and marquetry vase, displayed at the Ecole de Nancy Exposition, Paris, 1903

125
L'Orge, applied bronze-mounted ewer, displayed at the Ecole de Nancy Exposition, Paris, 1903

126
Passereaux Bleus, pair of applied scent bottles, displayed at the Ecole de Nancy Exposition, Paris, 1903

Plates 127–153:
Marquetry glassware

127
Marquetry vase inspired by the corolla of an ipomoea and moths, inscribed 'Echappez-vous des ombres immobiles – Leconte de l'Isle', Exposition Universelle, 1900

128
Marquetry and applied Etude vase, inscribed 'Gallé étude', 12¾in (32.4cm) high

129
Four marquetry vases decorated with
colchicums and crocuses

130
Applied and marquetry marine vase, inscribed
'La Patine des Verres', Exposition Universelle,
1900

131
Marquetry iris vase, 9¼in (23.5cm) high

132
Chardon des Alpes, marquetry vase, Exposition
Universelle, 1900

133
Fruit d'Iris, marquetry bottle with stopper,
Exposition Universelle, 1900

134
Selection of marquetry vases, c.1897

135
Flambé d'Eau, marquetry and applied vase,
Exposition Universelle, 1900

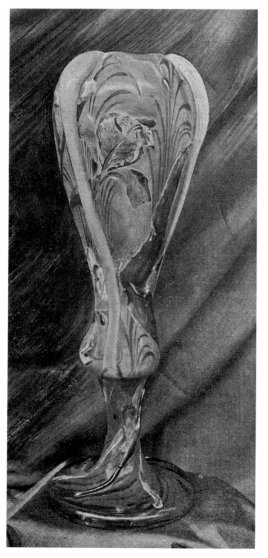

136
Les Safrans d'Hiver, a selection of marquetry vases decorated with crocuses, *c.*1897

137
Les Lumineuses, marquetry orchid vase, Exposition Universelle, 1900

138
Marquetry, applied and engraved vases

139
Marquetry vase, 5¼in (13.5cm) high

142
Marquetry vase, 5in (12.5cm) high

139
Marquetry vase, 5¼in (13.5cm) high

Selection of marquetry vases, *c*.1901

142
Marquetry vase, 5in (12.5cm) high

143
Marquetry butterfly vase, 13⅝in (34.6cm) high

144
Marquetry vase, Exposition Universelle, 1900

145
Vase with marquetry and applied onion
flower decoration, Exposition Universelle,
1900

Marquetry vase with applied decoration

Iris marquetry vase, 8¼in (21cm) high

148
Iris et Libellule, marquetry and applied vase
(the same model was exhibited at the 1900
Exposition Universelle), 15⅜in (39cm) high

150
Two marquetry vases, c. 1903

a   b

151
Two marquetry vases: (*a*) marquetry, applied
and *intercalaire* vase, 17⅞in (45.5cm) high;
(*b*) marquetry, engraved and *verre parlant* vase,
inscribed 'Petits sourires et grandes larmes –
Maeterlinck', 21½in (54.5cm) high

152
Gallé logo carried by the firm's salesmen to
advertise the technique of *marqueterie sur verre*

153
Marquetry vase, 7¾in (19.7cm) high

Plates 154–162:
Verreries parlantes

154
Cameo vase with applied grapes, inscribed 'Les globes, fruits vermeils des divines ramées – Victor Hugo', Exposition Universelle, 1900

155
Vase with applied tadpoles and inscribed 'Aux fossés la lentille d'eau de ses feuilles vert de grisées étale le glauque rideau (Theophile Gautier)', Exposition Universelle, 1900

156
Marquetry and cameo vase inscribed 'Toutes les âmes sont prêtes, mais il faut que l'une d'elles commence. Pourquoi ne pas être celle qui commence? (Maurice Maeterlinck)', Exposition Universelle, 1900

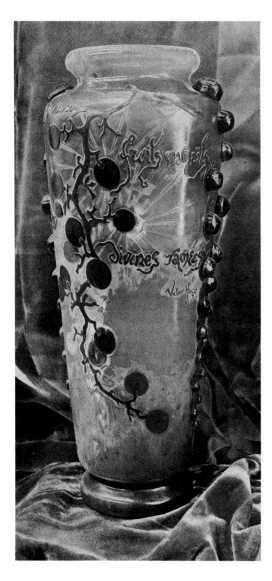

157
Marquetry vase inscribed 'Nous monterons enfin vers la lumière – Th. de Banville', c.1903

158
Cameo vase, 12⅝in (32cm) high, inscribed 'Béni soit le coin sombre où s'isolent nos coeurs – Valmore'

159
Marquetry vase, 20¼in (51.5cm) high, inscribed 'Mais le sabbat sombre aux rauques bluées a fui la fôret, le clair chant du coq perce les nuées ciel! L'aube apparaît. Victor Hugo', Exposition Universelle, 1900

160
Engraved glass vase, 4⅛in (10.5cm) high,
inscribed 'Par dessus la colline, Par dessus la
vallée Shakespeare Paris Exposition 1889'

161
Eaux Dormantes, engraved covered urn, 7in
(18cm) high, displayed at the Société
Nationale des Beaux-Arts, Paris, 1891, dated
1889–90 and inscribed
    '"La frisonnante libellule
    Mire le globe de ses yeux
    Dans l'étang splendide où pullule
    Tout un monde mystérieux" V. Hugo'

162
Carved and applied vase, inscribed 'Echappez-
vous des ombres immobiles', Exposition
Universelle, 1889 (the model was also
produced with the inscription 'Nul Souci de
Plaire')

Plates 163–167:
Glassware with imitation
hardstones and agates

163
Simulated moss agate vase, displayed at the
Salon Nationale des Beaux-Arts, Paris, 1904.
Now in the Musée de l'Ecole de Nancy, its
name is believed to be 'Géologie'

164
Imitation agate vase, 6½in (16.5cm) high

165
Two imitation hardstone vases: (*a*) amber;
(*b*) agate; 1890s

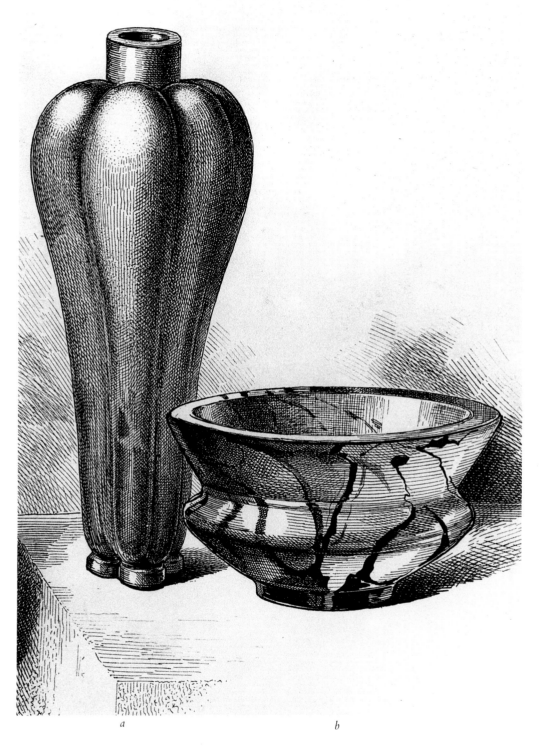

a   *b*

166
Engraved sang-de-boeuf bowl, 5⅛in
(13.4cm) high

167
Engraved sang-de-boeuf vase, 5½in
(14cm) high

Plates 168–178:
Verres hyalites and *vases de tristesse*

168
Selection of *vases de tristesse* displayed at the
Salon Nationale des Beaux-Arts, Paris, 1892

169
Rive Lacustre, engraved vase, Salon du
Champ-de-Mars, 1904

170
Sang-de-boeuf hyalite vase, 13¾in (35cm) high

171
Sang-de-boeuf hyalite vase, 6¾in (17cm) high

172
Sang-de-boeuf hyalite vase, 7in (17.6cm) high

173
Engraved marine vase, Exposition Universelle,
Paris, 1900

174
Orphée et Eurydice, engraved *verre parlant*
crystal vase designed by Victor Prouvé and
displayed at the Exposition Universelle, 1889.
Originally in the collection of M. Léon Clery,
now in the Musée des Arts Décoratifs, Paris

175
Engraved hyalite vase, 8¾in (22cm) high

176
Les Feuilles des Douleurs Passées, engraved vase,
Ecole de Nancy Exposition, Paris, 1903

177
Engraved and applied marine vase, Ecole de
Nancy Exposition, Paris, 1903

178
Engraved marine vase, Ecole de Nancy
Exposition, Paris, 1903

Plates 179–201:
Mounted glassware

179
Marquetry vase with bronze foot, 19$\frac{3}{8}$in
(49.4cm) high

180
Crystal vase with silver mount by Fabergé,
presented to the Russian Grand Duke, Sergé,
*c.*1896

181
Engraved glass vase with bronze foot,
Exposition Universelle, 1889

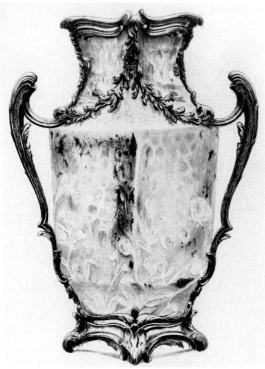

182
Vase in rose crystal, the silver-gilt mount
designed by Messagé and executed by M.
Froment-Meurice, Exposition Universelle,
1889, now in the Musée des Arts Décoratifs,
Paris

183
Saint Graal, crystal vase with elaborate silver-
gilt mount by Falize, *c.*1895

184
Scarabée gourd with bronze mounts, displayed
at the Ecole de Nancy Exposition, Paris, 1903

185
Silver-mounted etched and enamelled flaçon,
6in (15.5cm) high

186
Cameo vase with gold mount
by Falize, presented to the
Empress of Russia, 1896

187
Marquetry vase with bronze
mount by Bonvallet, illustrated
in *Art et décoration*, 1902

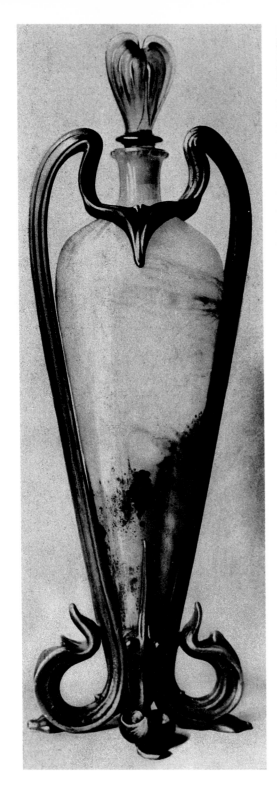

188
Bottle with wrought-iron mount, illustrated
in *Art et décoration*, 1903

189
Silver-mounted cameo vase, 17in (43cm) high

190
Cameo vase with wood base, *c.*1900

191
Cameo vase with carved wood base,
c.1900

192
Carved cameo bottle and stopper with silver-gilt mounts, 6⅛in (25.4cm) high; and carved ewer with silver-gilt handle, 5⅞in (15cm) high

193
L'Etoile du Matin, l'Etoile du Soir, Victor Hugo,
applied and marquetry vase with bronze
mount, *c.*1902

194
Sketch for a Gallé vase showing an elaborate
flowerform mount

195
Le Chêne, marquetry vase with bronze mount,
presented to the Empress of Russia, *c.*1896

196
*Heureux les Pacifiques Car ils Possédent la Terre,
St Mathieu*, marquetry vase with bronze
mount, *c.*1902

197
L'Orge, bronze-mounted pitcher, Ecole de Nancy Exposition, Paris, 1903

198
Neiges de Pentecôte, marquetry vase with bronze foot, collection of M. Germain Bapst, Exposition Universelle, 1900

199
Répos dans la Solitude, marquetry vase, collection of Count Foulon de Vaux, Exposition Universelle, 1900. The mount appears to be wood

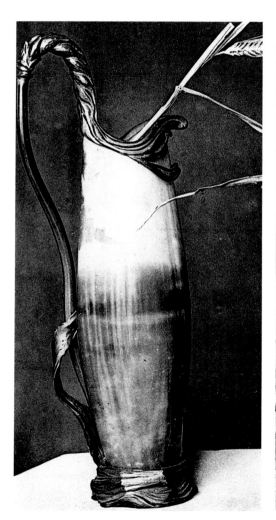

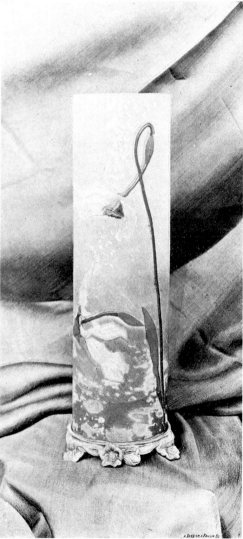

200
Marquetry vase with gilt-bronze foot, 7½in
(19cm) high

201
Silver-mounted cameo perfume burner, 6½in
(16.5cm) high

Chapter nine

Lamps

It is unclear why Gallé was not more drawn to lamps as a medium for his art. Perhaps the early uncertainty about the commercial future of electricity was a sufficient deterrent; the spluttering, feeble yellow glow of the early light bulb was hardly a trustworthy vehicle by which to promote one's work. Whatever the reason, lamps did not form a significant part of Gallé's repertoire in glass; no mention was made of them in his 1884 and 1889 Notes, and only brief reference in 1892 and 1900. Only in the last two years of his life does it appear that Gallé realized the full aesthetic potential of glass viewed by transmitted light. Of the relatively few non-commercial examples to have survived, none is disappointing. Posthumous models, if anything, use the medium more effectively. Double- and triple-layered cameo table lamps, chandeliers, sconces and night lights utilize the brilliance of electricity with magical effect. Many collectors today place a light bulb inside industrial vases to highlight the subtleties of the superimposed translucent layers of glass.

Though lamps did not feature prominently in Gallé exhibits at either the salons or international expositions, one exception was *La Solanée*, shown in 1900, its lace-like petalled shade inscribed with a verse by Victor Hugo, 'La lumière montera dans tout comme une sève.' At the 1903 Pavillon de Marsan there was a selection of graceful table lamps and chandeliers etched with bats, lilies and the ubiquitous umbel plant. A year later, at the Ecole de Nancy exhibition, two further important examples were introduced: *Les Coprins*, which is discussed elsewhere, and *La Fleur de Palmier*, an uncharacteristic depiction of a palm bough, its shade composed of strings of bead-like blossoms falling from the curved bronze stem.

A favourite lamp motif was cow parsley, an umbel indigenous to Lorraine. Existing records of the Gallé firm show that umbel lamps frequently incorporated the flower on the base *only*; the shade was decorated with butterflies as an

overall floral design was found to be overwhelming. This fact
often causes collectors incorrectly to question whether the
shade and base of these models are perfectly matched.

According to the recollections of René Dézavelle, the model
of the bat lamp, today a highly prized Gallé item, was
originally designed with a swarm of black butterflies, their
wings haloed with gold and silver, above a line of silhouetted
black trees on the lower shade. Very few models sold. Dr
Perdrizet determined that this was because the black butterflies
symbolized neurasthenia, a disorder generating insomnia and
headaches! They were therefore replaced by the flight of a
beautiful bat so that the tree-line would represent dusk against
the orange-red background. This effect, in turn, was found to
be too dismal and the idea was quickly dropped. Hence the
rarity of this much sought-after work of art!

One unique commission was a floor lamp retained by the
Gallé family. A metre wide, the etched shade depicted twenty
green and yellow parakeets perched on the flowering branches
of a gingko (maidenhair tree) against a pale orange sky. The
bronze mounts were cast as gingko branches.

The date of manufacture of the major Gallé cameo lamps –
such as the wisteria, chrysanthemum, peony, lemon tree and
laburnum models – appears to be unrecorded. Of formidable
size with large domed shades on baluster bases, the three- or
four-layered designs are strikingly beautiful, often with dabs of
colour applied on the interior of the shade to emphasize flower
centres or buds. The red and purple rhododendron lamps,
every bit as stunning, were exhibited at the 1925 Exposition
Universelle.

Chapter ten

Acid-etching

Gallé began experimenting with acid-etching in the mid-1880s to supplement the time-consuming technique of wheel-engraving. He carefully listed the limitations of the process in his Note to the Jury at the 1889 Exposition:

> Certainly, if acid could have saved me unnecessarily slow work in outlining prominent motifs by hollowing out the background, I would not have hesitated to use it, since in the end what matters in a work of art is the final result. My work, however, involves a material which is no longer in its pure state, but made up of superimposed layers of different density, composition and thickness, the behaviour of which the craftsman cannot predict before he cuts into them. You can therefore understand that the slightest touch by a blind agent [i.e. acid] could ruin everything, and that nothing can replace the hand of an artist who knows what he wants.

Etching was not a technique that would enhance Gallé's artistic reputation. One exhibit, a small four-layered vase decorated with pink roses on a black, brown and white ground, was described in the firm's catalogue solely as 'cameo'. It was probably an early example of wheel-engraving used in conjunction with etching, the latter's presence carefully disguised by the engraver in his touching up operation.

However, the consummate artist was forced to transform himself into a pragmatic businessman. Only by mass-producing an inexpensive range of commercial glassware could Gallé raise the capital necessary to keep the firm in business. The key to this was acid-etching. In 1906, Roger Marx drew attention to the fact that the very same problem had forced Gallé to industrialize his cabinetry workshops in 1894. Marx wrote in *La Revue universelle: littérature et beaux-arts* of the two-tier quality of Gallé's furniture: 'Whereas a select number of pieces were designed for museums, others were vulgar, commercial and industrial, assembled with measured economy to reach every home.' The sad reality was that the revenue generated by Gallé's commercial glassware and furniture was indispensable to the firm's operation, in large part subsidizing the disproportionate time and artisanship spent on experimentation and *pièces uniques*. So despite Gallé's aversion to a process that lacked the precision and artistic dexterity required of the manual operation, acid-etching was in full commercial use by the mid-1890s. Numerous etched pieces were illustrated in monthly art reviews, particularly *Deutsche Kunst und Dekoration* and the *Magazine of Art*, the former presenting a selection of cameo table lamps which showed that Gallé, like many of his contemporaries, had no ready solution at first to the unsightly tangle of light sockets and cord which carried power to the newly discovered *fée électricité*.

Few etched pieces were evident in Gallé's stand at the 1900 Exposition Universelle; in that year *marqueterie de verre* and patination were his newest discoveries and warranted pride of place. An exception, however, was *Endormeuses Saisons*, designed by Louis Hestaux on a theme from Baudelaire. This piece appears from a contemporary photograph to have been entirely etched. Gallé's etching process was described in the scientific journal *La Nature* in 1913. Fundamentally unchanged from its introduction roughly twenty-eight years earlier, it remained in operation until the firm's closure in 1931. Today such pieces are generally referred to as 'industrial Gallé'.

Once the choice of colours for a series of vases had been made, batches of each were placed in separate crucibles in a Boëtius coke-burning furnace and heated to melting point (1400°–1450°). The first colour was then gathered on a pipe and blown onto the marver where it was rolled flat. The second colour was similarly gathered and rolled on top of the first. Each additional colour – seldom more than four – was superimposed in this manner.

The layered mass of glass was then re-heated and blown into a wooden mould. This, fashioned in the cabinet-maker's shop, was made of two hinged sections which were opened when the shaped vase (all mould-blown items, such as bowls, lamp shades and bases, were similarly manufactured) had been slowly annealed in the lehr.

The vase was next transferred to a draughtsman-decorator who traced the chosen motif – usually floral or a continuous landscape – onto it with an indelible white pencil, carefully indicating which parts were to be retained by etching, and which not.

For large editions, especially after 1918, the procedure was standardized. The design, sketched beforehand by a master designer, was transferred onto a transparent wax pattern paper which was pierced with tiny holes. The pattern paper was then wrapped around the vase and a white powder sprinkled onto it and rubbed into the holes. When the paper was removed, the outline of the design was visible on the glass surface, providing the decorator with a key by which to apply his acid-resistant paint. The application of the powder, paint and acid, followed by polishing as a final step, took roughly one and a half days for each piece of glass. In his early experiments with the process, Gallé had three similar designs made up, from which he would, after lengthy examination, retain one and destroy the others. Examples of the pattern paper can be viewed at the Corning Museum of Glass and the Ottawa Museum.

The vase was now ready for one of the *verriers*, seated on stools in long rows lining the brightly lit *atelier*. Heavy vases were assigned to the men and lighter ones to the women. Each *verrier* was equipped with a mug of Judean bitumen (a resinous acid-resistant paste), brushes and rags. The vase was positioned on a wooden bar and secured with one hand while the liquid bitumen was applied with a brush to mask out the parts to be retained. It was then immersed in a large lead-lined bath of hydrofluoric acid. The progress of the acid as it ate its way into the surface of the glass was carefully monitored, its *agressivité* ('biting power') determined in the laboratory beforehand to match the hardness of the glass. Next, the vase was removed from the bath and washed and dried before being returned to the *verrier* for a further application of bitumen.

This process was repeated until each successive layer had been thinned down, penetrated in spots or totally removed. Finally, the vase was transferred to a polisher to be buffed on an emery wheel. This removed defects such as ragged edges, mould seams and remaining traces of acid. Certain pieces, for special effect, would be given a final diluted acid bath to give the etched ground a matt finish, followed by a buffing on a putty-coated cork wheel to provide the raised surface with a highly mirrored finish, thus increasing the contrast between the primary and secondary areas of design. This technique is today commonly referred to as 'wheel polishing'.

Gallé's industrial glassware varies widely in quality. Early pieces, especially, were superbly rendered, to the extent that they are often almost indistinguishable from wheel-carved examples in their sharpness of detail and subtle colour gradations.

Gallé's initial dislike of the process gave way to guarded approval as his *verriers* mastered the nuances of the acid bath. Special effects were introduced. The veining of leaves and pitting of tree trunks soon seemed more realistic than nature, as did the light grisaille patterning which could be applied to backgrounds. A charming variation were random flower sprays etched on the *interior* of a vessel or lampshade, surprising and delighting the viewer.

The process's main function was, however, to produce a huge volume of commercial wares, such as table lamps, chandeliers, brushholders and vases, at competitive prices. Consequently, most pieces were by definition of average quality, hurried through the factory to retail outlets in Frankfurt, Paris and London.

Chapter eleven

Mould-blown glassware

The term 'mould-blown' or 'soufflé' is generally used today to distinguish between Gallé industrial glassware which has relief detailing and that which does not. Whereas in both instances the shape of the vessel was formed in a mould, in a mould-blown piece the primary decoration protrudes from the surface to provide increased definition and realism.

The technique was limited almost exclusively to a series of cameo vases and light fixtures decorated with vegetables and fruit, to which it was well suited. Apples and pendant bunches of cherries stand out naturalistically against pale matt skies, each domed piece of fruit highly polished and with internal luminosity. Others in the series included plums, crocuses, tulips, tomatoes, hyacinths, fuchsias, water lilies, morning glories and rambler roses. Fruit-laden orange and lemon branches embellish the underside of a pair of chandeliers; on another a squirrel forages for acorns on an oak bough. The most expensive mould-blown model today is the rhododendron table lamp, produced with either red or purple blossoms.

Two layers of glass were selected for most mould-blown pieces, more sophisticated designs receiving three. The technique was the same as that used for standard industrial wares – hydrofluoric acid – colours within editions being interchanged to extend the range of effects.

It was assumed until recently that the process was introduced during Gallé's lifetime, or soon thereafter. However, *Ecrits pour l'art*, published posthumously in 1908, makes no mention of this kind of relief surface decoration, a most uncharacteristic omission for the fastidious Gallé, whose concern with precedence drove him to tabulate all his inventions. The mystery was solved in M. Dézavelle's 1974 speech: the entire mould-blown series was introduced, well after Gallé's death, in the years 1924–25, in time for the 1925 Exposition Universelle, where a wide selection was displayed. Included was that most peculiar of Gallé items, the 'elephant' vase.

Chapter twelve

The glassworkers

Alsace-Lorraine was richly endowed in glass tradition; the vast forests of the neighbouring Vosges region provided glasshouses with the fuel necessary to heat their furnaces. Beyond Nancy, the ancestral seat of power, the industry had spread south-east to Lunéville, north to Longwy and Metz, and north-east to Meisenthal, the last-mentioned annexed in 1871 by Germany following the Franco-Prussian war. Nearby, also, were St Louis in the Moselle region and St Quircin and Laon.

An army of artisans, their skills interchangeable, serviced the numerous glasshouses. Apprenticeship in one was often followed by a fresh start elsewhere. Armed with his new qualifications, a journeyman artisan might well effect a brighter career where his early, perhaps uncelebrated, training was unknown. There was, therefore, a lively traffic between glasshouses, one which accelerated as a firm's economic fortunes rose and fell from year to year in the battle for state and private commissions. It was from this itinerant labour force that Gallé first had to search for workers. Soon his rapid accomplishments and reputation for even-handedness drew the province's finest directly to the gates of 39 avenue de la Garenne. From this élite the team was picked which would complete experiments that, in turn, propelled Gallé toward new discoveries. The number of employees quickly swelled as early successes brought increased commissions. In 1883 Roger Marx indicated in the *Nancy Artiste* the speed with which the glassworks was expanding. He wrote that Gallé had 'under his direction a pleiad of artists. Prouvé made his first essays there, Uriot and Hestaux work there, the young sculptor Jacquot has recently joined; they find themselves in a milieu which greatly contributes to the development of the artistic fibre which they all possess. And I ask myself if one should envy Gallé for employing such artists or if it is not better to congratulate these youngsters for having such a master as their leader.'

By 1889, the number of glass artisans was listed as 300.

View of the glassworks with artisans, *c*.1904

Included under the broad heading of *verriers* were designers, enamellers, engravers, etchers, polishers, chemists and blowers, all supported by teams of apprentices and unskilled aides. Stocktakers, packers and shippers completed the count.

Part of Gallé's genius lay in his ability to share the credit with his collaborators. Though always effectively in command – designing or overseeing the multiplicity of projects underway simultaneously within the plant – he realized that individual ambitions had to be catered to, that egos had continually to be massaged. He managed this with more self-confidence than many. Tiffany, for example, tried to keep the names of his designers and glass artists a virtual secret for fifty years, leading several top window designers to branch out on their own.

Understandably, the names of Gallé's earliest employees were not as well documented as those of the heady 1900–04 years when the international art community turned its full gaze on every facet of Gallé's life and work. The earliest collaborator was, of course, Victor Prouvé, whose ubiquitous talents were soon drawn upon freely by all of Nancy. In the 1880s came Louis Hestaux (1858–1919), Uriot (1852–?) and Marcellin Daigueperce (?–1896). Hestaux, in particular, appears from the start to have been accorded a special place, and was credited with numerous works in glass and furniture throughout a long and distinguished employment. Most of the glass artists who helped in Gallé's *tours de force* at the turn of the century joined the firm in the early to mid-1890s, many in 1894 when the new glassworks opened. These included Albert Daigueperce (Marcellin's son), Emile Munier, Julien Roiseaux and Paul Holderbach, all mentioned by Dr Gustav Pazaurek in his 1901 *Moderne Gläser* for their contribution to Gallé's success at the 1900 Exposition Universelle. Several employees, in fact, were awarded individual prizes by the Jury at the exhibition, including Louis Hestaux, Auguste Herbst, and the chemist, Daniel Schoen.

Gallé inspecting the glassworks, *c*.1904

Gallé examining the progress of a glassblower and gaffer

137

A section of the works with Gallé's office in the centre

The catalogues for the 1903 and 1904 Ecole de Nancy Expositions in Paris and Nancy list the firm's foremost glass artists as follows:

Director:	Emile Lang
Painters:	Louis Hestaux, Paul Nicolas, Paul Holderbach
Glass Masters:	Gillet, Roiseaux, Meyer, etc.
Chief Decorator:	Emile Munier
Engravers:	Ismaël Soriot; Schmitberger; Mlle Rose Wild; Mercier, *père et fils*; Lang, *père*

For the daily administration of the works, Gallé drew, among others, on Clara Moeller (?–1893) and on his father, Charles Gallé (1818–1902). Many artisans stayed on after Gallé's death, some to the First World War, others to the firm's closure.

In 1920 some of the older decorators faithful to the pure Gallé tradition rebelled against the avalanche of industrial wares under production and set up their own small workshop. Under the supervision of Emile Nicolas, blank *vases en double* (two-layered glassware) were commissioned from the nearby St Louis glasshouse. These were decorated by Windeek and Villermeaux and then etched by Florentin to be marketed under the trade name 'D'Argental'. Bankruptcy forced the enterprise to close, Villermeaux and Florentin returning to their previous employment at the Gallé works.

Above right: two of a set of four marquetry panels on a Gallé vitrine at the Conservatoire National des Arts et Métiers, Paris. Designed by Auguste Herbst, a cabinet-maker in the furniture department, they depict various stages in the glassmaking process. Gallé can be seen in the lower panel instructing a decorator on the design required. *Right*: the industrial glass department, *c*.1900. Charles Gallé is standing on the left

Removing rough edges on an emery wheel. A high finish was obtained by changing to a cork wheel coated with emery powder, *c.*1914

The application of acid-resistant Judean bitumen to larger glassware (*above*) and to smaller pieces, *c.*1914

Chapter thirteen

The post-Gallé industrial era (1905–31)

Following Gallé's death, his widow, Mme Henriette Gallé, placed the direction of the firm under Dr Paul Perdrizet, her son-in-law. She explained her decision to keep the firm in business in a circular to clients:

> I have the honour to inform you that, following the sad death of my husband, with whose works I have always been associated, I have made the decision to retain all his employees; designers, modellers, engravers, sculptors and artisans. With the help of these devoted collaborators and thanks to the inexhaustible collection of projects and studies accumulated by Gallé himself, I will continue to produce the works of art and the techniques which have made him renowned . . .

On Mme Gallé's death in 1914, an article in *L'Etoile de l'Est* explained that this decision in 1904 had been taken solely to preserve the livelihood of the workers, whose numbers had swollen to 450 by 1914, double that of 1901.

Gallé's 1889 truce with industrial production, hugely reluctant but pragmatic, became the firm's post-1904 charter:

> You will see from my glassware that art and taste do not depend on costly methods of manufacture: what is needed is that one adjust one's designs with grace and feeling to meet the economic and technical limitations at hand. In my low-cost goods, I have avoided the false, the over-elaborate and the fragile by using sound colours and a large range of new designs to influence public taste. I have shown the way for glass-makers, and have demonstrated (sometimes to my own disadvantage) how factories can go in for mass-production on a very large scale.

Quality was downgraded as costs were pared. The lavish four- and three-layered cameo models of yesteryear were largely eliminated; retained were a series of two-layered pieces

141

depicting flora and landscapes. Large vases were manufactured in editions of ten dozen; *bonbonnières* and small vessels in twenty- to thirty-dozen editions. Shortly before the First World War a series of vases were decorated with panoramas of the Vosges mountain chain and the Gérardmer, Longemer and Retournemer lakes. The vases were engraved with a defiant, jingoistic slogan that would soon return to haunt Germany: 'This vessel, decorated with the gold and blue of the Vosges mountains, from where arise the lamentations of the vanquished, symbolizes the loss of Alsace-Lorraine in 1870.' Not surprisingly, when the models were reissued in 1918, the inscription was deemed redundant and therefore removed.

Two-colour permutations for scenic vases evolved: landscapes with perennials, lakes and mountains were in blue; those with bushes, trees and meadows were in green. A popular blue model was the 'Lake Como' vase, inspired by a watercolour that one of the designer-decorators painted on a holiday in northern Italy. In the foreground, beneath a eucalyptus tree, was a balustrade on which a peacock strutted. Beyond was Lake Como; in the distance a shadowy blue mountain range. A similar edition, depicting the bay at Rio de Janeiro with Sugarloaf Mountain in the background, was made for the American and English markets.

After 1918, a muted, autumnal palette was preferred: grey, green, brown, amber and burgundy. There appears to have been only one surprise: a series of 'polar bear' vases in opaque white on a translucent sapphire-blue ground, the sharply angular ice floes indicating their 1920s Art Deco genesis.

The factory closed at the beginning of the First World War, reopening after the armistice. Dr Perdrizet, joined now in the firm's management by Gallé's two other sons-in-law, Messrs Chevalier and Bourgogne, decided to concentrate production on a series of smaller glassware; large items had proved to be too costly and did not sell well. Their decision to manufacture assembly-line items only was no doubt sound; without the guiding genius and inspiration of its creator, no other course was commercially viable for the firm. Some romantics will decry the fact, however, that the firm did not remove Gallé's name from its wares after 1904; others that it did not summarily close its doors, providing posterity with a clean chapter in glassmaking history.

The Gallé firm closed in 1931, the glass workshops being converted into a technical school for electricians. The magasin de la rue de la Faiencerie, which had always carried Gallé's wares, continued to do so until 1935. In the same year, Eugène Corbin made the donation which established the Lorraine Museum of Modern Decorative Arts, today Le Musée de l'Ecole de Nancy.

Chapter fourteen

Exhibitions

Gallé participated in numerous exhibitions, both local and international, from the 1860s (ceramics) until the 1904/05 Ecole de Nancy exhibition, in the second month of which he died.

The annual salon of the Société Nationale des Beaux-Arts in Paris was the usual forum where critics and competitors were introduced to his new experimentation. Major developments – *marqueterie de verre*, patination, etc. – were shown as they were perfected rather than held for the large international exhibitions which punctuated the period.

The Gallé firm continued to participate after 1904 in Ecole de Nancy exhibitions until the latter's dissolution prior to World War I. After 1918 the firm's history is sketchy: certainly a major exhibit was mounted at the 1925 Exposition Universelle; thereafter firm records list participation in regional fairs – for example, Lyons and Leipzig.

Major Gallé Glass Exhibitions

1878   Exposition Universelle, Paris
        Classe 19 (Cristallerie, Verrerie, Vitraux)

1884   VIIIᵉ Exposition de l'Union Centrale des Arts
        Décoratifs, Paris
        (Theme: Les Arts de la pierre, du bois, de la terre,
        et du verre)
        Salon des Artistes Lorrains, Galerie de la salle Poirel,
        Nancy

1885   Exposition de la Loterie Nancienne, rue Saint-Dizier,
        Nancy

1889   Exposition Universelle, Paris
        Groupe III, Classe 19 (Cristallerie, Verrerie,
        Emaux)

1891   Salon des Artistes Français, Paris
        Salon de la Société Nationale des Beaux-Arts,
        Champ-de-Mars, Paris

1892   Salon de la Société Nationale des Beaux-Arts,
        Champ-de-Mars, Paris

1893   World's Fair, Chicago

1894   Salon de la Société Nationale des Beaux-Arts,
        Champ-de-Mars, Paris
        Exposition d'Art Décoratif et Industriel Lorrain,
        Nancy

1895   Salon de la Société Nationale des Beaux-Arts,
        Champ-de-Mars, Paris

1896   Salon de Nancy, Nancy

1897   8. Internationale Kunstausstellung, Munich
        Salon Internationale des Beaux-Arts, Brussels
        Konst-och Industriutsällningen, Stockholm
        Salon de la Société Nationale des Beaux-Arts,
        Champ-de-Mars, Paris

1898   Salon de la Société Nationale des Beaux-Arts,
        Champ-de-Mars, Paris

1900   Exposition Universelle, Paris
        Classe 73 (a. L'Histoire du verre français, Pavillon
        de l'Union Centrale des Arts Décoratifs; b.
        Exposition Centennale Rétrospective des Arts du
        XIXᵉ siècle, Musée Centennal; c. Cristallerie
        française contemporaine, Pavillon de l'Union
        Centrale des Arts Décoratifs)
        Exposition des Arts Appliqués, Bordeaux

1901   Exposition de la Maison d'Art Lorraine, Nancy
        Deutsche Kunstgewerbe Ausstellung, Dresden

1902   Salon de la Société Nationale des Beaux-Arts,
        Champ-de-Mars, Paris
        Exposition Internationale des Arts Décoratifs
        Modernes, Turin

1903   Salon de la Société Nationale des Beaux-Arts,
        Champ-de-Mars, Paris
        Exposition de l'Ecole de Nancy, Pavillon de Marsan,
        Paris

1904   Salon de la Société Nationale des Beaux-Arts,
        Champ-de-Mars, Paris
        Ecole de Nancy Exposition d'Art Décoratif, XLIᵉ
        Exposition de la Société Lorraine des Amis des
        Arts, Nancy

1908   Exposition de l'Ecole de Nancy, Palais de Rohan,
        Strasbourg

1925   Exposition Internationale des Arts Décoratifs et
        Industriels Modernes, Paris

Plates 202–252:
Lamps

202
Hibiscus cameo table lamp, 28in (71cm) high

203
203
Cameo table lamp, 13¼in (33.5cm) high

204
Cameo *plafonnier* with wrought-iron mount,
18in (45.5cm) overall height

205
Cameo table lamp, 21in (53cm) high

206
Cameo table lamp, 21in (53.5cm) high; and
bronze-mounted veilleuse, 10in (25.5cm) high

207
Three cameo table lamps

208
Magnolia cameo table lamp, 32in (81cm) high

209
Bronze-mounted cameo table lamp, 18in (45.5cm) high, base attributed to Peter Tereszczuk

210
Two cameo lamps: $15\frac{1}{2}$in (39.5cm) high; and 22in (56cm) high

a   *b*

211
Cameo table lamp, 8¾in (22cm) high

213
Corolla cameo table lamp with gilt-bronze
mount, 13½in (34.5cm) high

214
Peony cameo table lamp, 25in (63.5cm) high

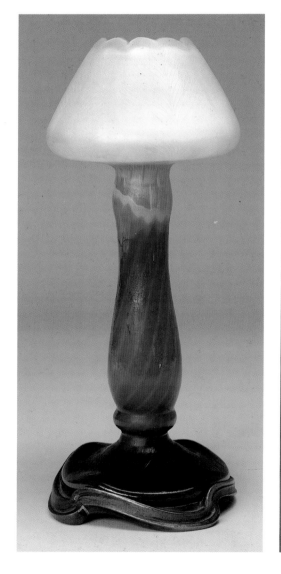

Cameo table lamp, 19in (48cm) high

218
Morning glory cameo table lamp, 11¼in
(28.5cm) high

219
Rhododendron mould-blown cameo table
lamp, 19in (48.5cm) high

Sketch of a selection of lamps and glassware
displayed by Gallé at the Exposition of the
Société Lorraine des Amis des Arts, Nancy,
1904. The second lamp from the left is
entitled *La Fleur de Palmier*, behind it is a
marquetry centrepiece, *La Nature*

Guéridon with table lamp, Ecole de Nancy
Exposition, Paris, 1903

222
La Solanée, table lamp inscribed 'la lumière montera dans tout comme une sève. Victor Hugo', 1900

223
Les Coprins, table lamp on *Les Ombellules* guéridon, displayed at the Exposition of the Société Lorraine des Amis des Arts, Nancy, 1905

224
Table lamp designed as an iris pod with bronze mount, Exposition Universelle, 1900

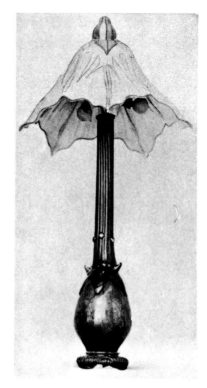

225
Two cameo table lamps, illustrated in *Deutsche Kunst und Dekoration*, 1904

226
Cameo table lamp, 10½in (26.5cm) high

227
Cameo table lamp, 14½in (37cm) high

228
Orange cameo table lamp, 32in (81cm) high

229
Cameo table lamp, 21in (53.5cm) high

230
Table lamp, *c*.1902

231
Selection of etched lamps and chandeliers
displayed at the Exposition of the Société des
Amis des Arts, Nancy, 1904

232
Selection of cameo table lamps and
chandeliers displayed at the Ecole de Nancy
Exposition, Paris, 1903

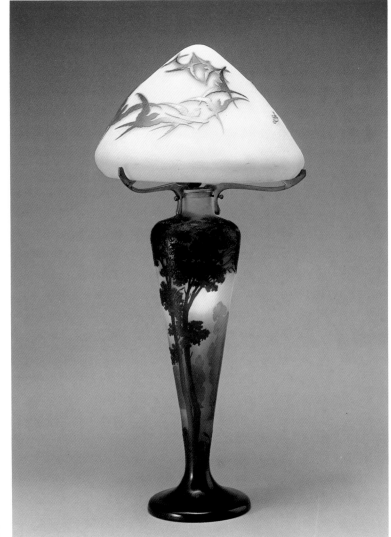

235
Cameo table lamp, 15¾in (40cm) high

236
Cherry mould-blown cameo table lamp,
18½in (51.6cm) high

Three table lamps with metal mounts, Ecole
de Nancy Exposition, Paris, 1903

238
Metal-mounted perfume burner and a table
lamp, *c.*1904

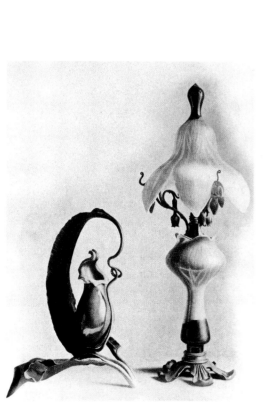

167

241
Pair of cameo table lamps, 15in (38cm) high

242
Two cameo chandeliers with gilt-bronze mounts, 19in (48.5cm) height to ceiling; and a cameo table lamp, 20⅛in (51.6cm) high

243
Cameo table lamp, 15in (38cm) high

244
Orange mould-blown cameo chandelier, 19½in (49.5cm) diameter

245
Cameo table lamp, 27in (68.5cm) high

246
Cameo table lamp, 23in (58.5cm) high

247
Cameo table lamp, 20¾in (52.5cm) high

248
Cameo table lamp, 19½in (49.5cm) high

249
Cameo table lamp, 17½in (44.5cm) high

250
Cameo table lamp, 26½in (67cm) high

251
Cameo glass and wrought-iron table lamp,
21¾in (54cm) high

252
Bat cameo glass and bronze-mounted table
lamp, 13⅜in (33.7cm) high

254
Etched and enamelled vases

255
Cameo vase, 20¼in (51.5cm) high

256
Cameo vase, 16½in (40.5cm) high

257
Two cameo vases

258
Three cameo vases, the centre one mould-blown

259
Cameo bowl, 10¼in (26cm) diameter

260
Cameo handled bowl, 11in (28cm) long

263
Cameo vase, $17\frac{1}{2}$in (44.5cm) high
264
Cameo vase, 33in (84cm) high

265
Three cameo vases

266
Four vases: (*a*), (*c*) and (*d*) etched, (*b*) with silver mount

a   b   c   d

267
(*a*) engraved cameo vase, $6\frac{1}{2}$in (16.5cm) high;
(*b*) marquetry vase, 4in (10cm) high; (*c*) engraved cameo vase, $5\frac{1}{4}$in (13.5cm) high

a   b   c

268
Cameo vase with highly polished finish, 18in
(45.5cm) high

269
Cameo marine vase with highly polished
finish, 4⅜in (11cm) high

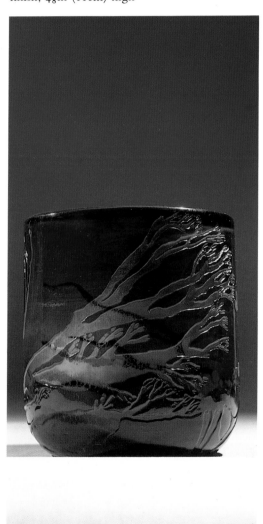

270
Cameo vase, 16½in (42cm) high

271
Cameo vase, 8in (20.5cm) high

272
Cameo jardinière, 16in (40.5cm) long

273
Le Bouleau, cameo vase, Exposition
Universelle, 1900

274
Endormeuses Saisons, designed by Louis
Hestaux on a theme from Baudelaire,
Exposition Universelle, 1900

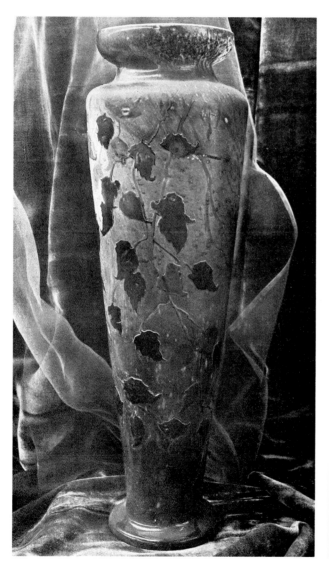

275
(a) cameo vase, 8⅛in (20.6cm) high; (b) metal-mounted cameo vase, 5⅝in (14.3cm) high

276
Cameo glassware: (a) 11½in (19cm) high; (b) 10in (25.5cm) high; (c) clematis, mould-blown vase, 9½in (24cm) high

a   b

a   b   c

278
Selection of cameo vases, 1903

279
Selection of cameo glassware, 1903

280
Three cameo vases: (*a*) *verre parlant* vase inscribed 'Les arbres se parlent tout bas. Victor Hugo', 17¾in (45cm) high; (*b*) 15¾in (40cm) high; (*c*) *verre parlant* vase inscribed 'Ubi Geritas et Justitia ibi Libertas à S.A.F. Madame le Comtesse d'Eui pour ses chers Villages de Liberté d'Afrique 1902', 15¼in (39cm) high

a   *b*   *c*

281
Five cameo vases

282
Cameo vase with simulated moss agate
ground, 7½in (19cm) high

283
Cameo vase, $10\frac{1}{8}$ in (25.7cm) high

285
Selection of cameo vases, most 1890/1900

287
Selection of cameo vases, 1890/1900s

288
Three cameo vases

289
Cameo glass vase, 24½in (62.3cm) high

290
Two cameo vases, both 20¼in (51cm) high

291
Cameo dish, 16⅜in (41.5cm) high

Plates 292–302:
Mould-blown glassware

292
Mould-blown vases: tulip, $13\frac{1}{2}$in
(34cm) high; wild rose, $9\frac{1}{2}$in (24cm)
high; and cherry, $10\frac{5}{8}$in (27cm) high

293
Two grape mould-blown vases, 11in
(28cm) high

294
Clematis mould-blown vase, 6¾in (17cm) high

295
Apple blossom mould-blown vase, 13$\frac{3}{8}$in (34cm) high

296
Mould-blown vases: fuchsia, $11\frac{3}{4}$in (30cm) high; clematis, $6\frac{1}{2}$in (16.5cm) high; and cherry, $11\frac{1}{2}$in (29cm) high

297
Marine mould-blown bowl, 7in (18cm) high, $12\frac{3}{4}$in (32.5cm) diameter

298
Two mould-blown vases: clematis, $9\frac{1}{2}$in (24cm) high; and plum, $15\frac{3}{5}$in (39.5cm) high

299
Mould-blown vases: morning glory,
10in (25.5cm) high; and apple, 11¾in
(30cm) high

300
Pair of hyacinth mould-blown vases,
12in (30.5cm) high

301
Mould-blown vases: cala lily, 14¼in
(36cm) high; and elephant, 15¼in
(38.5cm) high

302
Plum mould-blown vase, 13in (33cm) high

304
Cameo vase dipicting Lake Como, 13¾in
(35cm) high

305
Cameo vase, 10⅞in (27.5cm) high

Plates 308–320:
View of Gallé's exhibits

308
Les Fougères, vitrine enclosing a selection of glassware, Salon de la Société Nationale des Beaux-Arts, Champ-de-Mars, 1902

309
La Vigne Blanche, buffet with a selection of glassware, Exposition Universelle, 1900

310
Selection of glassware at an exhibition in Nancy, *c.*1897

311, 312
Two views of the Gallé exhibit in the Ecole
de Nancy pavilion, Nancy, c.1903

313
Selection of glassware at the Musée des Arts
Décoratifs, Nancy, 1890s

314
Gallé's exhibit at the Salon de la Société
Nationale des Beaux-Arts, Champ-de-Mars,
Paris, 1893

315, 316
Two views of the Gallé exhibit at the
Exposition Universelle, 1900

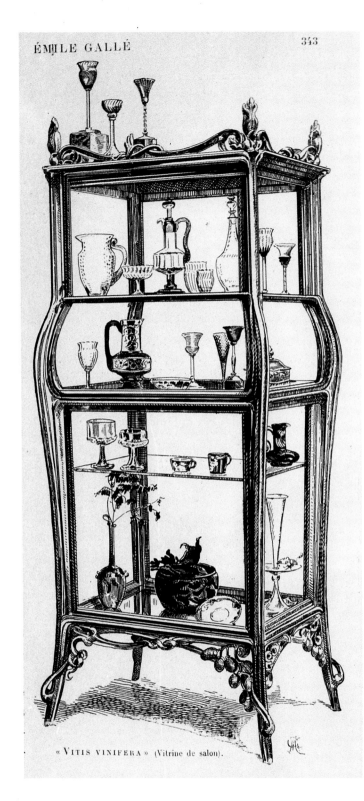

ÉMILE GALLÉ   343

« VITIS VINIFERA » (Vitrine de salon).

317
Vitrine with glassware in Gallé's exhibit at the Ecole de Nancy exposition at the Musée des Arts Décoratifs, Paris, 1903

318
Gallé's glass furnace at the Exposition Universelle, 1900. Several well-known models are visible

319
Gallé's kiosk at the Exposition Universelle,
1889

Signatures

Surviving sketches show that Gallé himself designed the signatures for his glassware. Explicit notations for the engraver, etcher or enameller defined their means of execution. The number of signature permutations is endless, each an inspired response by the master to the work at hand, each in itself an enchanting miniature work of art.

Signatures can be divided chronologically into three broad periods which help to determine when a piece was made. The first is 1868–85, when most glassware was transparent. Signatures were frequently engraved or traced in black or gold ink. Often the signature is incorporated in a larger and more complex design including a Cross of Lorraine, dedication, or epithet, all carved on a pansy or clover leaf.

In the second period – 1886–1904 – the firm's glassware was largely opaque. Signatures on pieces created under Gallé's personal supervision became fanciful renditions of the Art Nouveau style. Some are simple, others so configured that they are hard to decipher. Invariably, the signature matches the design on the vase: an elongated cursive script running diagonally across the lower half of the piece complements the swaying flowers above, or an overlapping blocked signature echoes the theme of a vase's Japanese ideogram. Exposition pieces are often identified as such and dated; others are signed with a variation of *Déposé* ('patent applied for') or *Gallé me fecit*, the Latin for 'Gallé made me.' Industrial glassware in the same period carried relatively simple etched signatures as it did in the third era, 1904–31.

A signature preceded by a star has been understood generally to indicate that the piece was made sometime between Gallé's death in 1904 and the advent of the First World War, the period when the firm was under the direction of Gallé's widow. However, information from M. Dézavelle has shown this not to be true. In fact, the starred signature was used only between 1904 and 1906 as a tribute to the master following his death. One reason why it was so short-lived was no doubt that the market reacted negatively to pieces identified as posthumous.

Gallé glassware was invariably signed, though early inked signatures are sometimes today barely visible, effaced through time by repeated handling. There are three possible reasons for the absence of a signature. The first, and most likely, is that it has been removed, probably because the immediate area on the glass was chipped. The second is that the piece is not by Gallé but by a competitor, such as D'Argental or Delatte, whose glassware is often indistinguishable from the Gallé firm's late 1920s industrial production. By removing the lesser known and important signature, an enterprising Gallé entrepreneur has hoped to increase the value of the piece. And the third and least likely reason is that the piece carries only the name of the retailer – *L'Escalier de Cristal*, for example, who provided metal mounts for a range of Gallé glass. What the absence of a signature does *not* mean is that it is a rare 'unsigned' piece!

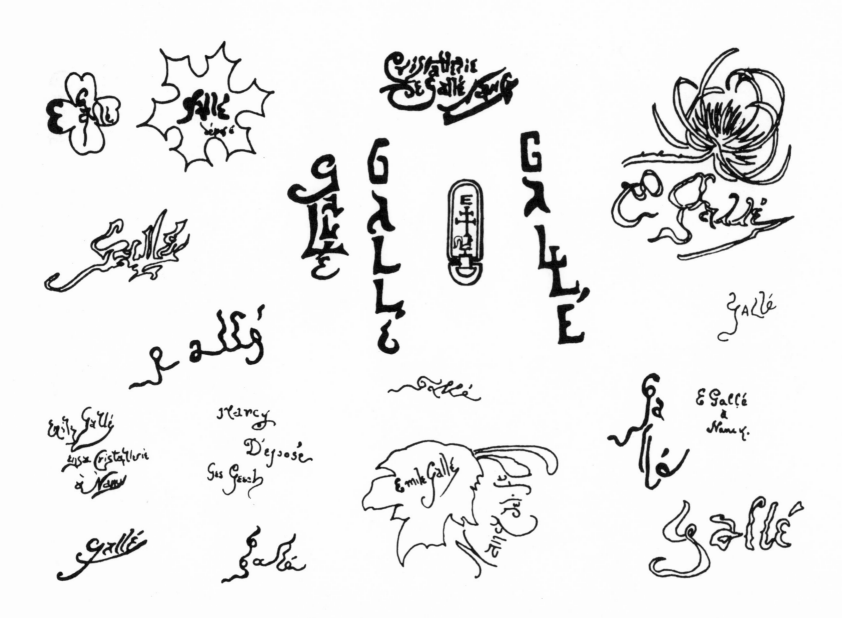

Prices

The prices for Gallé glassware have followed a proven cycle. In 1903, at the height of his fame, the *Libellule* coupe cost 350 f. The same invoice to an important Belgian client lists an *Orchidée* vase at 300 f. An article some years later in *La Gazette des beaux-arts* states that Gallé's industrial glass could be purchased for as little as 3 f., no doubt for the smallest of etched wares. The difference in price between the firm's best and worst was, therefore, immense; a gap that, however, has widened even further today as certain collectors pursue only the aesthetic pinnacle of Gallé's production, pushing the value of top pieces ever upwards.

In 1914, at the Paris auction of Roger Marx's estate, a selection of extremely fine carved and sculpted pieces brought incredibly modest prices, a combination of the economic austerity and uncertainty of the immediate pre-war era and the general demise of Art Nouveau. The firm's loose-leaf catalogue for the 1925 Exposition Universelle provides an invaluable guide to its prices for industrial glassware at the time. The large cameo table lamp decorated with either an orange or lemon tree, 31in (78.74cm) high, cost $350; a 24in (60.96cm) high floral or landscape model cost roughly $150. The newly introduced series of mould-blown vases – decorated in relief with tomatoes, cherries, apples, etc. – ranged in price from $40 to $100. In this series, the clematis vase cost $58 and the marine bowl $96. Among standard cameo vases illustrated in the catalogue, the 'Lake Como' model was listed at $120, higher, surprisingly, than the mould-blown series.

Until the late 1950s, prices were unspectacular and often indiscriminating. A Brussels dealer recalls with amusement drawing a circle on the floor in his gallery and charging a set amount for all the Gallé glassware that a client could cram into it! The Art Nouveau renaissance in the 1960s drew the first of a host of books on the subject, helping to underline both the importance of Gallé's works and the distinction in workmanship between his different techniques. Prices began to vary accordingly, those for the masterworks accelerating quickly to rarified levels. By the end of the 1970s, the value of certain top pieces, such as the *Rhubarbe* coupe sold at Christie's in Geneva, had exceeded $200,000. Others which sold privately, such as the *Coprins* lamps and the 'King Solomon' amphora vase, have demanded twice that amount. At the lower end of the scale, prices for small cameo pieces, such as the 1920s two-layered industrial ware, have flattened out, showing little fluctuation from season to season.

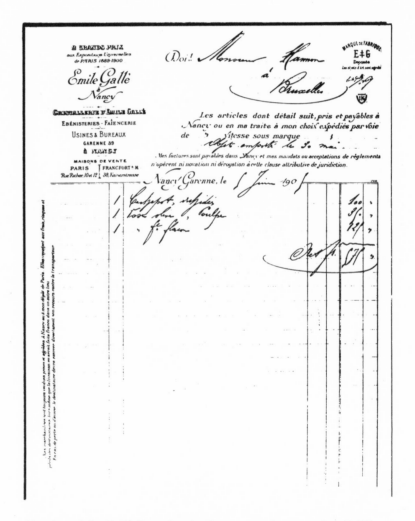

Invoice of the Gallé firm, dated 5 June 1905, the year after Gallé's death, when prices were still relatively high. A cache-pot and two vases cost 571 f.

Bibliography

General

L'Art décoratif, 1902–14
La Revue alsacienne illustrée, 1905–09
Le Monde moderne
Le Bulletin de la Société d'Horticulture de Nancy
La Gazette des beaux-arts, 1888-1912
La Lorraine Artiste
La Revue des arts décoratifs, 1888-1901
Art et industrie, 1909–12
La Revue artistique et industrielle, 1900
La Revue de l'art, 1897–1912
La Revue de l'art ancien et moderne, 1897–1904
Le Bulletin des Sociétés Artistiques de l'Est
La Revue lorraine illustrée, 1905–09
Art et decoration, 1888–1910
L'Art décoratif aux salons, 1898–1906
Deutsche Kunst und Dekoration, 1897–1907
International Studio, 1890–1905
Les Arts, 1902–12
Kunst und Handwerk, 1898–1904

Specific

ARWAS, VICTOR, *Glass: Art Nouveau to Art Deco* London, 1977, pp. 73–101

BARRELET, JAMES, *La Verrerie en France* Paris, 1953, p. 175

BLOCH-DERMANT, JANINE, *The Art of French Glass, 1860–1914* London, 1980, pp. 52–134

Catalogue des objets d'art moderne: La Collection Roger Marx Auction catalogue, Galerie Manzi, Joyant, l'Eveque, Paris, 13 May 1914, pp. 66–106

CHARPENTIER, F.-T., *Emile Gallé* Nancy, 1978

DEMORIANE, HÉLÈNE, 'Le Cas étrange de Monsieur Gallé' in *Connaissance des arts* 1960 (102) pp. 35–41

DÉZAVELLE, RENÉ, 'The History of the Gallé Vases' in *Glasfax Newsletter* 1974 (6) entire issue

DUNCAN, ALASTAIR, *Art Nouveau and Art Deco Lighting* London, 1978, pp. 77–78

GALLÉ, EMILE, *Ecrits pour l'art* Paris, 1907

GARNER, PHILIPPE, *Emile Gallé* New York, 1976

GILLET, LOUIS, 'Emile Gallé, la poète du verre' in *Revue hebdomadaire* 1910 (October) pp. 153ff

GROS, GABRIELLA, 'Poetry in Glass: The Art of Emile Gallé, 1846–1905' in *Apollo* 1955 (369) pp. 134–36

HAKENJOS, BERND, *Emile Gallé, Keramik, Glas und Mobel des Art Nouveau* Inaugural diss., University of Cologne, 1982

HOFMAN, H. D., 'Emile Gallé and Louis Majorelle' in *Kunst in Hessen und am Mittelrhein* 1968 (8) pp. 65–75

HONEY, W. B., 'A Forgotten Artist in Glass: Emile Gallé of Nancy' in *Antique Collector* 1947 (January–February) pp. 25–26

KARAGEORGEVITCH, B., 'Emile Gallé: A Master of Glass' in *Magazine of Art* 1904 (May) pp. 310–14

LANORVILLE, GEORGE, 'Les Cristaux d'art d'Emile Gallé' in *La Nature* 1913 (1 March) pp. 209–13

MARX, ROGER, 'Conférence sur Emile Gallé' in *L'Art social* Paris, 1913, pp. 111–51

MEIXMORON, CHARLES DE, *Réponse au récipiendaire, memoires de l'Academie de Stanislas, 1889–1900* Nancy, 1901

PAZAUREK, DR GUSTAVE E., *Moderne Gläser* Leipzig, 1901

POLAK, ADA, *Modern Glass* New York, 1962, pp. 31, 85

———, 'Signatures on Gallé Glass' in *Journal of Glass Studies* 1966 (8) pp. 120–27

Revue encyclopédique, La 1893 (59) pp. 481–84; 1893 (62) pp. 635–40; 1894 (92) pp. 426–28

SCHRIJER, ELKA, *Glass and Crystal II* New York, 1964, pp. 22–23

THIOLÈRE, EDOUARD, 'Les Etablissements Emile Gallé à Nancy' in *La Revue industrielle de l'Est* 1906 (11) pp. 278–83

TISSERAND, ERNEST, 'La Poème en verre d'Emile Gallé a René Lalique' in *Art vivant* 1925, pp. 722–31

Acknowledgments

Gratitude is extended to the following for their assistance in the compilation of this book:

Félix Marcilhac, Mme F.-T. Charpentier, Stephen Koo, Mrs Areta Kauffman, William Warmus, Tom King, Mrs Chantal Ratcliffe, Mrs Amy Freedman Sharah, Dr Henry Blount, Sheila Harrison, Mme René Dézavelle and Jean-Loup Charmet

Index

Page numbers in *italic* refer to the illustrations in the text.